Themes
for Today

Themes
for Today

Second Edition

Reading For Today SERIES, BOOK 1

1

LORRAINE C. SMITH
Adelphi University

NANCY NICI MARE
English Language Institute
Queens College
The City University of New York

THOMSON

HEINLE

Australia • Canada • Mexico • Singapore • United Kingdom • United States

THOMSON

HEINLE

Themes for Today, Second Edition
Lorraine C. Smith and Nancy Nici Mare

Publisher, Adult and Academic ESL: *James W. Brown*
Senior Acquisitions Editor: *Sherrise Roehr*
Development Editor: *Sarah Barnicle*
Senior Production Editor: *Maryellen E. Killeen*
Senior Marketing Manager: *Charlotte Sturdy*
Director, Global ESL Training & Development:
  Evelyn Nelson
Senior Print Buyer: *Mary Beth Hennebury*

Compositor: *Parkwood Composition Service*
Project Manager: *Hockett Editorial Service*
Photo Researcher: *Susan Van Etten*
Photography Manager: *Sheri Blaney*
Illustrator: *Glenn Reid*
Cover Designer: *Ha Ngyuen*
Text Designer: *Carole Rollins*
Printer: *Edwards Brothers*

Printed in the United States of America
1 2 3 4 5 6 7 8 9 10   06 05 04 03

For more information contact Heinle, 25 Thomson Place, Boston, Massachusetts 02210 USA, or you can visit our Internet site at http://www.heinle.com

For permission to use material from this text or product contact us:

Tel	1-800-730-2214
Fax	1-800-730-2215
Web	www.thomsonrights.com

Library of Congress Control Number   2003106360

ISBN   0-88377-113-6
ISE ISBN   1413000754

For Tom

CREDITS

Photographs

p. 1, © Ariel Skelley/CORBIS
p. 2, © B. Kraft/© 1998CORBIS/Sygma
p. 6, © Gamma Press/GAMMA
p. 15, © Whitney Gray
p. 19, © Whitney Gray
p. 25, © José Luis Pelaez, Inc./CORBIS
p. 31, © Dallas & John Heaton/CORBIS
p. 32, © Bettmann/CORBIS
p. 37, © Tony Freeman/Photo Edit
p. 44, © Ed Quinn/CORBIS
p. 49, © Michael Newman/Photo Edit
p. 54, © Michael Newman/Photo Edit
p. 59, © Bill Aron/ Photo Edit
p. 61, © Jeff Zaruba/CORBIS
p. 67, © Donald Graham/Index Stock Imagery
p. 68, © Tom Stewart/CORBIS
P. 73, © José Luis Pelaez, Inc./CORBIS
p. 79, © Norbert Schaefer/CORBIS
p. 83, © Reuters NewMedia, Inc./CORBIS
p. 99, © Homer Sykes/Woodfin Camp & Associates
p. 100, © AP/American Museum of Natural History
p. 105, © Bettmann/CORBIS
p. 115, © Bettmann/CORBIS
p. 122, © Susan Van Etten
p. 129, © Chip Henderson/Index Stock Imagery
p. 135, © Steve Dunwell Photography, Inc./Index Stock Imagery
p. 136, © Susan Van Etten
p. 152, from: Santarem Atlas, In the Map Division, New York Public Library, Astor, Lenox and Tilden Foundations
p. 158, Model & photography© Joseph Tenga
p. 161, from: Nova Totious Terrarum, in the Map Division, New York Public Library, Astor, Lenox and Tilden Foundations
p. 171, © Reuters NewMedia, Inc./CORBIS
p. 172, © PhotoDiscRF/Getty Images
p. 176, © Reuters New Media, Inc./CORBIS
p. 188, © Vo Trung Dung/CORBIS
p. 194, © Hulton-Deutsch Collection/CORBIS
p. 201, © Reuters NewMedia, Inc./CORBIS

CONTENTS

Unit	Chapter and Title	Reading Skills Focus	Structure Focus	Follow-up Activities Skills Focus
CNN® Video Report and Internet Topics				
Unit 1 **Home and Family** **Page 1**	Chapter 1 **The McCaugheys: An Unusual Family** Page 2	• Preview reading • Understand True/False, Multiple Choice, Short Answer questions • Scan for information • Recall information • Identify main idea • Use context clues	• Identify parts of speech in context: nouns and verbs	• *Listening:* Evaluate spoken messages • *Writing:* Use a graphic organizer to organize ideas; write a schedule; write a list; write an opinion paragraph
• **CNN Video Report:** Homeschooling • **Internet Search:** Learning English as a Second Language	Chapter 2 **A Musical Family** Page 15	• Use a chart to answer questions • Understand True/False, Multiple Choice, Short Answer questions • Use context clues • Identify main ideas/details • Make inferences • Assert opinions about a reading	• Identify parts of speech in context: nouns and verbs	• *Listening:* Listen, take notes • *Writing:* Write a comparison/contrast paragraph; write a journal entry
Unit 2 **Language and Culture** **Page 31**	Chapter 3 **Learning a Second Language** Page 32	• Preview reading • Understand main ideas • Use background knowledge • Predict content • Use context clues • Use transitional expressions • Reflect on reading material • Scan for information • Identify the process • Identify the main idea • Draw conclusions	• Identify parts of speech in context: adjectives and adverbs • Recognize the suffix: *-ly*	• *Listening:* Evaluate the content of spoken messages • *Writing:* Use a graphic organizer; write a journal; write a letter
• **CNN Video Report:** The Changing Japanese Diet • **Internet Search:** Finding recipes; Learning about food in other cultures	Chapter 4 **Food and Culture** Page 49	• Share cultural experiences/ideas • Understand main idea • Scan for information • Recall information • Understand vocabulary • Understand True/False, Multiple Choice, Short Answer questions • Draw conclusions	• Identify parts of speech in context: nouns and verbs	• *Listening:* Listen and note opinions of others • *Writing:* Use graphic organizer to take notes; write a comparison-contrast paragraph; write a journal entry

Unit	Chapter and Title	Reading Skills Focus	Structure Focus	Follow-up Activities Skills Focus
CNN® Video Report and Internet Topics				
Unit 3 **Exercise and Fitness** Page 67	Chapter 5 **The Importance of Exercise for Children** Page 68	• Use the title to understand the main idea • Preview visuals to aid comprehension • Make inferences from text • Understand transitional words and phrases • Understand vocabulary from its context • Scan for information • Identify the main idea • Use personal experience to respond to a reading	• Identify parts of speech in context: nouns and verbs	• *Discussion:* Make recommendations to solve problems • *Writing:* Write a letter; write a journal entry
• **CNN Video Report:** Children's Health • **Internet Search:** Learn more about the New York Marathon; New exercises for health	Chapter 6 **The New York City Marathon: A World Race** Page 83	• Use photographs and titles to understand the main idea • Make predictions • Understand T/F, multiple choice, and short answer questions • Interpret a map • Read for supporting details • Identify the main idea • Understand vocabulary from its context • Scan for information • Interpret numerical information on a graph	• Identify parts of speech in context: nouns and verbs • Recognize the suffix: *-ment*	• *Writing:* Use personal experience to reflect on reading; make a list of suggestions; write a journal entry
Unit 4 **Remarkable Researchers** Page 99	Chapter 7 **Margaret Mead: The World Was Her Home** Page 100	• Preview chapter through visuals • Use photographs and titles to understand the main idea • Predict the chapter topic • Understand T/F, multiple choice, and short answer questions • Understand vocabulary from its context • Interpret maps	• Identify parts of speech in context: nouns and verbs • Recognize the suffixes: *-ance* and *-ence*	• *Discussion:* Interview others about their culture • *Writing:* Write a descriptive paragraph; take notes; write a journal entry
• **CNN Video Report:** Doctor and Humanitarian • **Internet Search:** Researching the researchers	Chapter 8 **Louis Pasteur: A Modern-Day Scientist** Page 115	• Preview chapter through visuals • Use titles to understand the main idea • Understand T/F, multiple choice, and short answer questions • Understand vocabulary from its context • Scan for supporting details	• Identify parts of speech in context: nouns and verbs • Recognize the suffix: *-tion*	• *Discussion:* Compare and contrast • *Writing:* Write an expository paragraph; write predictions with supporting examples; write a journal entry

Unit	Chapter and Title	Reading Skills Focus	Structure Focus	Follow-up Activities Skills Focus
CNN® Video Report and Internet Topics				
Unit 5 **Science and History** Page 135	Chapter 9 **The Origin of the Moon** Page 136	• Previewing • Understand T/F, multiple choice, and short answer questions • Understand vocabulary from its context	• Identify parts of speech in context: nouns and verbs • Recognize the suffix: -tion	• *Discussion:* Compare ideas; create a plan • *Writing:* Make a list; write an opinion paragraph; write a journal entry
• **CNN Video Report:** NASA Pictures of Space • **Internet Search:** Learn more about space and astronomy; View pictures of space	Chapter 10 **Maps: The Keys to Our World** Page 152	• Use titles to understand the main idea • Understand vocabulary from its context • Look at art and maps to assist reading comprehension • Understand content area vocabulary: maps and measurement	• Identify parts of speech in context: adjectives and adverbs • Recognize the suffix: -ly	• *Discussion:* Make and compare lists • *Writing:* Write a descriptive paragraph
Unit 6 **Future Technology Today** Page 171	Chapter 11 **Saving Lives with Weather Forecasting** Page 172	• Preview • Predict • Find the main idea using the title • Understand content area vocabulary: weather • Vocabulary in context • Scan for details • Open-ended question • Identify main ideas • Sequence events • Interpret charts	• Identify parts of speech in context: nouns and verbs • Recognize the suffixes: -ance and -ence	• *Listening:* Listen for information; share ideas • *Writing:* Write a journal entry
• **CNN Video Report:** Forecasting Hurricanes • **Internet Search:** Finding local weather forecasts; Learn more about weather	Chapter 12 **Clues and Criminal Investigation** Page 188	• Preview vocabulary • Predicting • Use the title to understand the main idea • Understand content area vocabulary: crime and forensics • Use content to understand vocabulary • Identify main ideas • Scan for information • Find supporting details • Find examples	• Identify parts of speech in context: nouns and adjectives • Recognize the suffix: -ful	• *Listening-Speaking:* Retell a news story • *Writing:* Solve problems and suggest solutions; write an opinion or persuasive paragraph, write a journal entry
	Index of Key Words and Phrases Page 207 **Skills Index** Page 211			

PREFACE

Themes for Today, Second Edition is a reading skills text intended for academically oriented students of English as a second or foreign language who have had at least some exposure to English. *Themes for Today* encompasses such areas as health, history, science, and technology. Experience has shown that college-bound students are interested in working with more academic subjects than are often found in ESL texts at the lower level. At the same time, beginning ESL students need to work with topics that they have some familiarity with—those topics for which they have some background knowledge to draw on.

Themes for Today, Second Edition is one in a series of reading skills texts. The complete series has been designed to meet the needs of students from the beginning to the advanced levels and includes the following:

- *Themes for Today*   beginning
- *Insights for Today*   high beginning
- *Issues for Today*   intermediate
- *Concepts for Today*   high intermediate
- *Topics for Today*   advanced

Themes for Today, Second Edition provides students with essential practice in the types of reading skills they will need in an academic environment. It requires students to not only read text, but also to extract basic information from charts, graphs, illustrations, and photographs. Beginning level students are rarely exposed to this type of reading material. Furthermore, the students are given the opportunity to speak and write about their own experiences, country, and culture in English, and to compare them with those of the United States and other countries. This text has real-life activities that give students specific tasks to complete. Furthermore, all four skills—reading, writing, speaking, and listening—are incorporated into each chapter.

This text consists of six units. Each unit contains two chapters that deal with related subjects. At the same time, though, each chapter is entirely separate in content from the other chapter contained in that unit. This format gives the instructor the option of either completing entire units or choosing individual chapters as a focus.

The opening illustrations and the initial exercise preceding each reading encourage the students to think about the ideas, facts, and vocabulary that will be presented in the passage. Discussing illustrations in class helps lower level students visualize what they are going to read about and gives them cues for the new vocabulary they will encounter. Working in groups to activate and discuss prior knowledge of a subject helps enhance reading comprehension.

Readers, especially beginning second language readers, vary considerably in their strategy use and comprehension monitoring activities. Some readers benefit more from focusing on reading one or two paragraphs at a time and checking their comprehension before continuing to read. Other readers may prefer to read an entire passage and then consider questions related to the reading. Consequently, in order to provide maximum flexibility, all the reading passages are presented in two formats: in sections and complete. When the reading is presented in sections, each segment is followed by questions on content and vocabulary. Where the reading is presented in its complete form, it is followed by questions on content that ask the reader for inferences, conclusions, opinions, and main ideas. With this dual format, the teacher and students have three choices: all the students may read the passage in segments, then read it in its entirety; all the students may read the passage completely first, then attend to the questions following each segment; or the students may each choose which format they prefer to read first, according to their own preferences and needs.

The exercises that follow the reading passage are intended to develop and improve reading proficiency (including the ability to learn new vocabulary from context) and comprehension of English sentence structure. The activities give students the opportunity to master useful vocabulary encountered in the articles through discussion and group work and lead the students to comprehension of main ideas and specific information.

Lower level language students need considerable visual reinforcement of ideas and vocabulary. Therefore, this text contains a great many illustrations. In addition, many of the follow-up activities are of the type that enable students to manipulate the information in the text and supplemental information. In fact, the teacher may want the students to use the blackboard to work on the charts and lists in the activities throughout the chapters.

Much of the vocabulary is recycled in the exercises and activities in any given chapter, as well as throughout the book. Experience has shown that beginning level students especially need repeated exposure to new vocabulary and word forms. Repetition of vocabulary in varied contexts helps the students not only understand the new vocabulary better, but also helps them remember it.

As the students work through the text, they will learn and improve reading skills and develop confidence in their growing English proficiency skills. At the same time, the teacher will be able to observe their steady progress towards skillful, independent reading.

While **Themes for Today, Second Edition** retains the overall format of the first edition, the authors have made several significant changes to the original book. The second edition contains a new unit on Home and Family and in that unit are two chapters with a focus on unusual families and homeschooling.

In addition to the new chapters, the second edition is now accompanied by a CNN video composed of video clips to complement the topic of one of the chapters in each unit. At the end of each unit, video activities accompany the video to assist students in their viewing comprehension.

Also new to **Themes for Today, Second Edition** are Internet Activities designed to encourage students with school or home access to the Internet to learn more about a topic they read about in their text.

All of these revisions and enhancements to *Themes for Today, Second Edition,* have been designed to help students improve their reading skills, to reinforce vocabulary encountered, to encourage interest in the topics they examined, and to develop confidence as they work through the text. All of these skills are presented to prepare students for academic work and the technical world of information they are about to encounter.

INTRODUCTION

How to Use This Book

Every chapter in this book consists of the following:

Prereading Preparation
Reading Passage in Segments with Reading Analysis
Complete Reading Passage
Scanning for Information
Word Forms
Vocabulary in Context
Follow-up Activities
Topics for Discussion and Writing
Crossword Puzzle
Cloze Quiz

There are CNN® video and Internet activities at the end of each unit as well as an Index of Key Words and Phrases at the end of the book.

The format of each chapter in the book is consistent. Although each chapter can be done entirely in class, some exercises may be assigned for homework. This, of course, depends on the individual teacher's preference, as well as the availability of class time. Classwork will be most effective when done in pairs or groups, giving the students more opportunity to interact with the material and with each other.

Prereading Preparation

This prereading activity is designed to stimulate student interest and provide preliminary vocabulary for the passage itself. The importance of prereading preparation should not be underestimated. Studies have shown the positive effect of prereading preparation in motivating student interest and in enhancing reading comprehension. In fact, prereading discussion of topics and visuals has been shown to be more effective in improving reading comprehension than prereading vocabulary exercises per se. Time should be spent describing and discussing the illustrations as well as discussing the prereading questions. Furthermore, the students should try to relate the topics to their own experience, and try to predict what they are going to read about. Students may even choose to write a story based on the chapter-opening illustration.

The Reading Passage with Reading Analysis

Each reading passage is presented in segments. As the students read the passage for the first time, they can focus on the meaning of each paragraph. This exercise requires the students to think about the meanings of words and phrases, the structure of sentences and paragraphs, and the relationships of ideas to each other. They also have the opportunity to think about and predict what they will read in the next paragraph of the reading. This exercise is very effective when done in groups. It may also be done individually, but groups give the students an excellent opportunity to discuss possible answers.

Reading Passage

Students should be instructed to read the entire passage carefully a second time and to pay attention to the main idea and important details.

Scanning for Information

After students have read the complete passage, they will read the questions in this exercise, scan the complete passage for the answers, and then write the answers in the spaces under each question. The last question in this section always refers to the main idea. When the students are finished, they may compare their answers with a classmate's. The pairs of students can then refer back to the passage and check their answers. The students may prefer to work in pairs throughout this exercise.

Word Forms

In order to successfully complete the word form exercises in this book, the students will need to understand parts of speech, specifically nouns, verbs, adjectives, and adverbs. Teachers should point out each word form's position in a sentence. Students will develop a sense for which part of speech is necessary in a given

sentence. Because this is a low-level text, the Word Form exercise simply asks students to identify the correct part of speech. They do not need to consider the tense of verbs or the number (singular or plural) of nouns.

Vocabulary in Context

This is a fill-in exercise designed as a review of the items in the previous exercises. The vocabulary has been highlighted either in the prereading or elsewhere in the chapter. This exercise may be done for homework as a review or in class as group work.

Follow-up Activities

This section contains various activities appropriate to the information in the passages. Some activities are designed for pair and small group work. Students are encouraged to use the information and vocabulary from the passages both orally and in writing. The teacher may also use these questions and activities as home or in-class assignments. Some follow-up activities help the students interact with the real world because they require the students to go outside the classroom to interview people or to get specific information. In this way, students are not limited to speaking, reading, or learning in the classroom.

Topics for Discussion and Writing

This section provides ideas or questions for the students to think about and/or work on alone, in pairs, or in small groups. It provides beginning students with writing opportunities appropriate for their ability level, usually at the paragraph level.

Crossword Puzzle

Each chapter contains a crossword puzzle based on the vocabulary used in that chapter. Crossword puzzles are especially effective when the students work in pairs. Working together provides students with an opportunity to speak together and to discuss their reasons for their answers.

If pronunciation practice of letters is needed, students can go over the puzzle orally: The teacher can have the students spell out their answers in addition to pronouncing the words themselves. Students invariably enjoy doing crossword puzzles. They are a fun way to reinforce the vocabulary presented in the various exercises in each chapter, and they require students to pay attention to correct spelling.

Cloze Quiz

The Cloze quiz is the passage itself with 10–20 vocabulary items focused on the previous exercises and question sections omitted. The Cloze quiz tests not only vocabulary but also sentence structure and comprehension in general. The students are given the words to be filled in the blank spaces.

CNN Video and Internet Activities

At the end of each unit are optional activities designed to accompany one of the topics presented in each unit. The authentic CNN® videos were chosen to continue concepts presented in the readings, to reinforce vocabulary learned, and to encourage individual interest as well as group discussion. The optional Internet activities provided encourage students to explore information learned in *Themes for Today* through the technology available to them at school, in the library, or at home.

Index of Key Words and Phrases

This section contains words and phrases from all the chapters for easy reference. It is located after the last chapter.

ACKNOWLEDGMENTS

We are grateful to everyone at Heinle, especially to Sherrise Roehr for her continued support and to Sarah Barnicle for her hard work and keen eye. Special thanks also go to our family and friends for their ongoing encouragement.

L.C.S. and N.N.M.

UNIT

1

HOME AND FAMILY

1

1

The McCaugheys: An Unusual Family

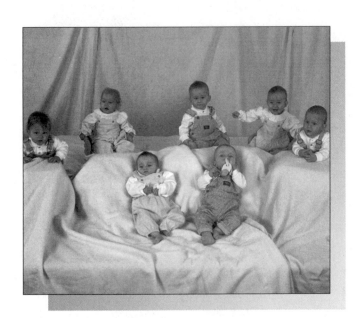

Prereading Preparation

1. Look at the picture. Work with a partner and answer the questions on the chart.

How many children are there?	How old are they?	Are they brothers and sisters?
Number _____	_____ months/years old	Yes or No

2. Read the title of this story. Why is this family unusual?

   a. They have young children.

   b. They have many young children.

   c. They have seven children the same age.

Directions: Read each paragraph carefully. Then answer the questions.

The McCaugheys: An Unusual Family

Kenny and Bobbi McCaughey live in Iowa. They have a big family. In fact, they have eight children. But this family is also very unusual. Mikayla is the oldest child in the family. She is 6 years old. The other children are Brandon, Joel, Kelsey, Kenny, Natalie, Alexis, and Nathan. They are all 5 years old. Why are they all the same age? Because they are septuplets! Septuplets are seven children who are born together.

1. Who are Kenny and Bobbi McCaughey?
    a. the parents
    b. the children

2. How many children do the McCaugheys have?
    a. eight
    b. seven
    c. five

3. What are **septuplets**?
    a. large families
    b. seven children born together
    c. 5-year-old children

4. _____ True _____ False   Mikayla is a septuplet.

5. How old are the septuplets? _____

It is hard work to take care of seven babies at the same time. But Kenny and Bobbi did not take care of the seven babies alone. In the beginning, many people helped them. The babies did not sleep a lot. So every day, eight or nine people came to the McCaughey house to help them. Their friends and families helped to feed, clean, and dress the babies. Every week, the septuplets used about 170 diapers! They drank a lot of milk, too.

6. _____ True _____ False   Many people helped Kenny and Bobbi.

7. ____ True ____ False   The septuplets slept a lot in the beginning.

8. Friends and families helped because septuplets
   a. are hard work
   b. drink a lot of milk
   c. are unusual

9. Babies use **diapers** because they
   a. can't drink from a cup
   b. can't use the bathroom

10. **Dress** means
    a. to put a dress on the babies
    b. to put clothes on the babies

Now the children are older. Bobbi says, "It's easier to take care of the children now. They feed and dress themselves, and they don't need diapers anymore!" The septuplets started school this year. But they do not leave the house. Why? The children go to school at home, like their big sister Mikayla. When Mikayla was ready for school, Kenny and Bobbi decided to teach her at home. "Homeschooling" is popular. Many families in the United States teach their children at home. The children do all their schoolwork at home. Last year, Bobbi was Mikayla's teacher. Now, Bobbi is the teacher for all eight of her children.

11. It's easier to take care of the septuplets now because
    a. they are older
    b. they go to school
    c. their big sister helps

12. The septuplets are unusual students because they
    a. go to school at home
    b. can't dress themselves
    c. are not ready to go to school

13. ____ True ____ False   The septuplets wear diapers now.

14. **Homeschooling is popular. Popular** means
    a. many people like homeschooling
    b. homeschooling is very expensive
    c. homeschooling is easy to do

15. Who is the septuplets' teacher? _____

16. What is **homeschooling**?
    a. Children do not learn.
    b. Children do not have teachers.
    c. Children learn at home.

Directions: Read the complete passage. When you are finished, you will answer the questions that follow.

The McCaugheys: An Unusual Family

1   Kenny and Bobbi McCaughey live in Iowa. They have a big family. In fact,
2   they have eight children. But this family is also very unusual. Mikayla is the old-
3   est child in the family. She is 6 years old. The other children are Brandon, Joel,
4   Kelsey, Kenny, Natalie, Alexis, and Nathan. They are all 5 years old. Why are they
5   all the same age? Because they are septuplets! Septuplets are seven children who
6   are born together.
7   It is hard work to take care of seven babies at the same time. But Kenny and
8   Bobbi did not take care of the seven babies alone. In the beginning, many people
9   helped them. The babies did not sleep a lot. So every day, eight or nine people
10 came to the McCaughey house to help them. Their friends and families helped to
11 feed, clean, and dress the babies. Every week, the septuplets used about 170 dia-
12 pers! They drank a lot of milk, too.
13   Now the children are older. Bobbi says, "It's easier to take care of the chil-
14 dren now. They feed and dress themselves, and they don't need diapers anymore!"
15 The septuplets started school this year. But they do not leave the house. Why?
16 The children go to school at home, like their big sister, Mikayla. When Mikayla
17 was reach for school, Kenny and Bobbi decided to teach her at home.
18 "Homeschooling" is popular. Many families in the United States teach their chil-
19 dren at home. The children do all their schoolwork at home. Last year, Bobbi was
20 Mikayla's teacher. Now, Bobbi is the teacher for all eight of her children.

A.   **Scanning for Information**

Read the following questions. Then go back to the complete passage and scan quickly for the answers. Write them in the space under each question.

1.   Where does the McCaughey family live? _____

2.   Who helped Kenny and Bobbi McCaughey take care of the septuplets?
     _____

3.   Why don't the septuplets wear diapers any more?
     _____

4.   Why don't the children go to school? _____

5.   The main idea of this story is:
     a.   It is hard work for parents to take care of septuplets.
     b.   Homeschooling is very popular today in the United States.
     c.   The McCaugheys are unusual because they have septuplets.

B.   Word Forms

In English, some words can be either a noun (n.) or a verb (v.), for example, *change*. Read the sentences below. Decide if the correct word is a noun or a verb. Circle your answer. Do the example below before you begin.

Example:

    a. We <u>change / change</u> our clothes every day.
            (v.)   (n.)

    b. The <u>change / change</u> in the weather made me sick.
             (v.)   (n.)

1. Kenny and Bobbi did not get very much <u>sleep / sleep</u> at first.
                                        (v.)   (n.)

2. The septuplets did not <u>sleep / sleep</u> very much at first.
                     (v.)   (n.)

3. Kenny and Bobbi's families <u>help / help</u> them with the children.
                        (v.)   (n.)

4. Kenny and Bobbi don't need a lot of <u>help / help</u> because the children are older.
                                 (v.)   (n.)

5. The family <u>uses / uses</u> a room in their house as a classroom.
             (v.)   (n.)

6. One room has many <u>uses / uses</u>! It is a classroom, a play room, and a living room.
                   (v.)   (n.)

7. Do you always <u>work / work</u> during the day?
             (v.)   (n.)

8. I do my <u>work / work</u> for school at night.
            (v.)   (n.)

9. The septuplets got a good <u>start / start</u> in life because so many people helped them.   (v.)   (n.)

10. I sometimes <u>start / start</u> my day by reading the newspaper.
               (v.)   (n.)

Vocabulary in Context

Read the following sentences. Choose the correct word for each sentence. Write your answers in the blank space.

> hard (*adj.*)　　helped (*v.*)　　septuplets (*n.*)　　together (*adj.*)

1. _____ are seven children who are born at the same time.

2. Brandon, Joel, Kelsey, Kenny, Natalie, Alexis, and Nathan are all 5 years old. They were born _____.

3. It is difficult to take care of seven babies. It is _____ work.

4. Many people _____ the McCaugheys. They cleaned and dressed the children.

> feed (*v.*)　　ready (*adj.*)　　unusual (*adj.*)

5. Every day, eight or nine people came to _____ the babies.

6. The McCaughey family is _____ because they have septuplets.

7. Children are _____ for school when they are 5 years old.

> decided (*v.*)　　popular (*adj.*)　　teacher (*n.*)

8. Bobbi and Kenny _____ to homeschool the children. They do not leave the house for school.

9. Homeschooling is _____ in the United States. Many people do it.

10. Bobbi is the _____ for all her children.

1. Work in a small group. The McCaugheys septuplets are 5 years old now. How much food do you think they eat in one day?

	Breakfast	Lunch	Dinner
Drinks			
Food			
Dessert			
Snacks			

2. Work in a group. Write a list of questions you want to ask the septuplets. Then exchange your list with another group. Try to answer their group's questions.

Questions	Answers
1.	1.
2.	2.
3.	3.
4.	4.
5.	5.

Topics FOR *Discussion* AND *Writing*

1. Bobbi is homeschooling her children. What subjects does she teach? Work in pairs and write a schedule for the McCaugheys' school day.

2. What will happen when the children are older? Will they go to school when they are teenagers? Or will Bobbi continue to homeschool them? What do you think? Share your ideas with your classmates.

3. Why do some people decide to homeschool their children? Think about some reasons and talk about them with your classmates.

4. Write in your journal. Do you think homeschooling is a good idea? Why or why not? Write a paragraph to explain this reason.

Crossword Puzzle

Read the clues on the next page. Then write the correct words on the puzzle.

Crossword Puzzle Clues

Across

3. The McCaugheys got _____ from their families and friends.

6. Only _____ child is not a septuplet.

8. The seven children were born at the _____ time.

10. _____ are seven children who are born at the same time.

11. Did Kenny and Bobbi _____ to teach the children at home? Yes!

13. When the septuplets were babies, they used 170 _____ every week.

14. Mikayla is _____ one of the septuplets.

16. The McCaughey family lives in _____. It is a state in the United States.

17. Bobbi is homeschooling her children. _____ is their teacher.

18. The children do not _____ to school. They study at home.

20. Mikayla is _____ than the septuplets.

Down

1. _____ of the children learn at home.

2. The septuplets can _____ themselves now. They can put on their clothes by themselves.

3. _____ is very popular in the United States and in other countries, too.

4. The seven younger children were born _____. They were born on the same day.

5. Teaching children at home is very _____. Many parents do it.

7. Septuplets are _____ children who are born at the same time.

9. Family and friends helped to _____ the children breakfast, lunch, and dinner.

12. Having eight children _____ a lot of work!

15. The McCaugheys are a very _____ family.

19. Feeding, dressing, and caring for eight children is _____ work.

Read the passage below. Fill in each space with the correct word from the list. Use each word only once.

alone	feed	hard	help	milk

It is _____ work to take care of seven babies at the same
            (1)
time. But Kenny and Bobbi did not take care of the seven babies

_____. In the beginning, many people helped them. The babies
         (2)
did not sleep a lot. So every day, eight or nine people came to the

McCaughey house to _____ them. Their friends and families
                          (3)
helped to _____, clean, and dress the babies. Every week, the
              (4)
septuplets used about 170 diapers! They drank a lot of _____, too.
                                                                      (5)

easier	leave	older	popular	ready

Now the children are _____. Bobbi says, "It's
                              (6)
_____ to take care of the children now. They feed and dress
         (7)
themselves, and they don't need diapers anymore!" The septuplets started

school this year. But they do not _____ the house. Why? The chil-
                                          (8)
dren go to school at home, like their big sister, Mikayla. When Mikayla was

_____ for school, Kenny and Bobbi decided to teach her at
         (9)
home. "Homeschooling" is _____. Many families in the United
                                 (10)
States teach their children at home. Now, Bobbi is the teacher for all eight of

her children.

2

A Musical Family

Prereading Preparation

Directions: Look at the picture. Read the title of the story. Then answer the questions.

Questions	Answers
1. What are these people holding?	
2. How many children are in the picture?	
3. What musical instruments do you see?	

Directions: Read each paragraph carefully. Then answer the questions.

A Musical Family

Shawn and Whitney Cabey-Gray lived with their four children in the city of Chicago. Every night, the family ate dinner together. Most of the time, the children talked about video games. The oldest child, Nick, did not like to talk about school. He was not doing well in math. Shawn and Whitney were very unhappy. They did not want this life for their children. Four years ago, they decided to make a change. What did they do?

1. Where did this family live? _____

2. Who are Shawn and Whitney?
   a. the parents
   b. the children

3. ____ True ____ False   The family played video games together every night.

4. ____ True ____ False   The family ate dinner together every night.

5. What did the children talk about at dinner? _____

6. Did Nick like to talk about school? _____

7. **Nick was not doing well in math** means
   a. he did not like math
   b. he did not get good grades in math
   c. he did good work in math

8. Why were Shawn and Whitney unhappy?
   a. They did not like to eat dinner together.
   b. They did not like to talk about video games.
   c. They did not like this life for the family.

9. **They decided to make a change. Decide** means
   a. make a choice
   b. talk about
   c. fight about

10. Answer this question: What did they do?

   _____

   Shawn and Whitney sold their house in Chicago. They threw away the video games and moved a thousand miles away to a very small town in Maine. Whitney decided to homeschool the children. Nick began to enjoy math. His schoolwork improved, and the other children's did, too.

11. Where did the family go? _____

12. _____ True _____ False   Maine is near Chicago.

13. Who is the children's teacher? _____

14. Why did Whitney decide to homeschool the children?
    a. She wanted to help them do better.
    b. She didn't like their teacher.
    c. The school was 1,000 miles away.

15. **Enjoy** means
    a. do
    b. work
    c. like

16. **Improve** means
    a. become harder
    b. become better
    c. become enjoyable

17. _____ True _____ False   The children's schoolwork improved.

All the children enjoyed their new lives, but sometimes they were bored. Shawn decided to give them music lessons. Now every afternoon, they play their music together. Each child plays a different musical instrument. Nick is 16 years old. He plays the viola. Zack, who is 13 years old, plays the cello. Twelve-year-old Bryanna, the only daughter in the family, plays the violin. The youngest child in the family is Noah. He is only 6 years old, but he plays the piano very well. In fact, he plays it better than his father! The children love to perform together, and Shawn and Whitney love to listen to them.

Now the Cabey-Gray family has a very different life. The town is quiet, but the Cabey-Gray's house is not!

18. **All the children enjoyed their new lives, but sometimes they were bored. Bored** means
    a. they had a lot of school work to do
    b. they did not have a lot of interesting things to do
    c. they did not have a lot of friends

19. Why did Shawn give them music lessons?
    a. The parents love to listen to the children.
    b. The children didn't enjoy their new lives.
    c. The children were bored.

20. Who is the oldest child? _____

21. Who is the youngest child? _____

22. How many daughters do Shawn and Whitney have? _____

23. **The children love to perform together** means
    a. the children love to play music together
    b. the children love to study together
    c. the children love to live in Maine together

24. Why isn't the Cabey-Gray's house quiet?

_____

Directions: Read the complete passage. When you are finished, answer the questions that follow.

A Musical Family

1   Shawn and Whitney Cabey-Gray lived with their four children in the city of
2   Chicago. Every night, the family ate dinner together. Most of the time, the chil-
3   dren talked about video games. The oldest child, Nick, did not like to talk about
4   school. He was not doing well in math. Shawn and Whitney were very unhappy.
5   They did not want this life for their children. Four years ago, they decided to
6   make a change. What did they do?

7   Shawn and Whitney sold their house in Chicago. They threw away the
8   video games and moved a thousand miles away to a very small town in Maine.
9   Whitney decided to homeschool the children. Nick began to enjoy math. His
10   schoolwork improved, and the other children's did, too.

11   All the children enjoyed their new lives, but sometimes they were bored.
12   Shawn decided to give them music lessons. Now every afternoon, they play their
13   music together. Each child plays a different musical instrument. Nick is 16 years

14 old. He plays the viola. Zack, who is 13 years old, plays the cello. Twelve-year-old
15 Bryanna, the only daughter in the family, plays the violin. The youngest child in
16 the family is Noah. He is only 6 years old, but he plays the piano very well. In
17 fact, he plays it better than his father! The children love to perform together, and
18 Shawn and Whitney love to listen to them.
19   Now the Cabey-Gray family has a very different life. The town is quiet, but
20 the Cabey-Gray's house is not!

Scanning for Information

Read the following questions. Then go back to the complete passage and scan quickly for the answers. Write them in the space under each question.

1. Why did the Cabey-Gray family move from Chicago to Maine?

   _____

2. What changes did the Cabey-Gray family make?
   a. _____
   b. _____
   c. _____

3. "All the children enjoyed their new lives, but sometimes they were bored. Shawn decided to give them music lessons." Why were the children bored?

   _____

4. How is the Cabey-Gray family's life different now?
   a. _____
   b. _____

5. What is the main idea of this passage?
   a. The Cabey-Gray children love to perform music together.
   b. The Cabey-Gray parents wanted their family to have a better life.
   c. The Cabey-Gray children's schoolwork improved a lot in Maine.

In English, some words can be either a noun (n.) or a verb (v.), for example, *work*. Read the sentences below. Decide if the correct word is a noun or a verb. Circle your answer. Do the example below before you begin.

Example:
a. I have a lot of <u>work / work</u> to do today.
       (v.)   (n.)

b. When I am busy, I <u>work / work</u> 10 or 11 hours in a day!
           (v.)   (n.)

1. The Lee family will <u>move / move</u> to Florida next month.
             (v.)   (n.)

2. They are very happy about the <u>move / move</u>.
                    (v.)   (n.)

3. The Cabey-Gray family decided to <u>change / change</u> their life.
                       (v.)   (n.)

4. The <u>change / change</u> was very important to the family.
         (v.)   (n.)

5. Shawn and Whitney <u>love / love</u> the children very much.
                 (v.)   (n.)

6. The children have a good life because of their parents' <u>love / love</u>.
                                (v.)   (n.)

Vocabulary in Context

Read the following sentences. Choose the correct word for each sentence. Write your answer in the blank space.

bored (*adj.*)   enjoyed (*v.*)   quiet (*adj.*)

1. The small town in Maine is a very _____ place to live.

2. The children became _____ because they did not have a lot to do.

3. After they moved, the children _____ their new lives in Maine.

improve (*v.*)   perform (*v.*)   unhappy (*adj.*)

4. Shawn and Whitney were _____ in Chicago. They did not like their lives.

5. The children like to play their musical instruments. They _____ together in their home.

6. Whitney homeschooled the children, and Nick's schoolwork started to _____.

decided (*v.*)   plays (*v.*)   lessons (*n.*)   threw away (*v.*)

7. Noah _____ the piano very well.

8. Bryanna _____ to play the violin, but Zack wanted to play the cello.

9. The parents _____ the children's video games. They did not want the children to play them anymore.

10. Shawn taught the children to play musical instruments. He gave music _____ to them.

1. In this chapter, the parents made a decision and changed their family's life. They moved 1,000 miles away from a big city to a small town. This is a very big change. Work in a group. Imagine you are Shawn or Whitney. You are unhappy, but you don't want to move far away. What other ways can you change your lives?

Changes in . . .	
our children's lives	
our lives	
our family's life	

2. The Cabey-Gray family moved to a different city. What changes did Shawn and Whitney make in their lives? Work with a partner, and make a list below.

Changes in Whitney's Life	Changes in Shawn's Life
1.	1.
2.	2.
3.	3.

Topics FOR *Discussion* AND *Writing*

1. The Cabey-Gray family moved from a large city to a small town. Do you want to live in a large city or a small town? Explain your answer.

2. Can you play a musical instrument? Write about it. Or write about a musical instrument you want to play.

3. Write in your journal. Do you think the Cabey-Gray family has a better life now? Why or why not?

Crossword Puzzle

Read the clues on the next page. Then write the correct words on the puzzle.

UNIT **1** Home and Family

Crossword Puzzle Clues

Across

4. A violin is a musical _____.

9. When we become better at something, we _____.

11. Make a choice

13. Noah is the _____ child in the family, and Nick is the oldest.

15. Noah plays _____ piano.

16. The opposite of quiet

17. In Chicago, the children played _____, but they don't play them in Maine.

Down

1. We feel _____ when we do not have something interesting to do.

2. Nick began to _____ math when his mother taught him. She made it fun!

3. The children sometimes _____ with their father—they are a five-person band.

5. Maine is a _____ miles from Chicago. They are very far from each other.

6. The Cabey-Gray family _____ from one home to a new home.

7. The family is _____ happy now.

8. Each child plays something _____. Nick plays the viola, Zack plays the cello, Bryanna plays the violin, and Noah plays the piano.

10. The children perform _____. They are a band.

12. Walk very fast

13. The opposite of "no"

14. In the Cabey-Gray family, _____ people play the piano: Noah and his father.

Read the passage below. Fill in each space with the correct word from the list. Use each word only once.

| began | enjoyed | improved | moved | sold |

Shawn and Whitney _____ their house in Chicago. They
             (1)
threw away the video games and _____ 1,000 miles away to a
             (2)
very small town in Maine. Whitney decided to homeschool the children. Nick
_____ to enjoy math. His schoolwork _____ , and
   (3)   (4)
the other children's did, too. All the children _____ their new
             (5)
lives, but sometimes they were bored.

| decided | different | only | together | youngest |

Shawn _____ to give them music lessons. Now, every
        (6)
afternoon they play their music _____. Each child plays a
            (7)
_____ musical instrument. Nick is 16 years old. He plays the
   (8)
viola. Zack, who is 13 years old, plays the cello. Twelve-year-old Bryanna, the
_____ daughter in the family, plays the violin. The
   (9)
_____ child in the family is Noah. He is only 6 years old, but he
   (10)
plays the piano very well.

1. The McCaughey and the Cabey-Gray families think homeschooling is a good idea. What do you think? In your opinion, why is homeschooling popular?

2. Read the statements below and then watch the video. Choose if the statements are true (T) or false (F).

   a. The Lynn family has two children. _____ T _____ F

   b. Diane Lynn teaches her children French, English, and other subjects. _____ T _____ F

   c. Rob Lynn has only been inside a school one time. _____ T _____ F

   d. The Lynn children never spend time with other children. _____ T _____ F

   e. Pat Montgomery thinks that homeschooling is good for everyone. _____ T _____ F

   f. Emily thinks homeschooling was good preparation for college. _____ T _____ F

3. What do you think about homeschooling? What are the advantages? What are the disadvantages?

 *Surfing* THE *INTERNET*

1. Go to the Internet and enter the address for a search engine such as **google.com**, **msn.com**, or **yahoo.com**.

2. Enter the search word *ESL* or search words *English as a Second Language* in the search engine.

3. Choose a website about **ESL**.

4. Print out a page and tell your class about the information you can find about **ESL** on the Internet. Will it help you study English? Share the address with your classmates.

Optional Activity: Read more information about homeschooling in other countries. Is it popular in other countries besides the United States?

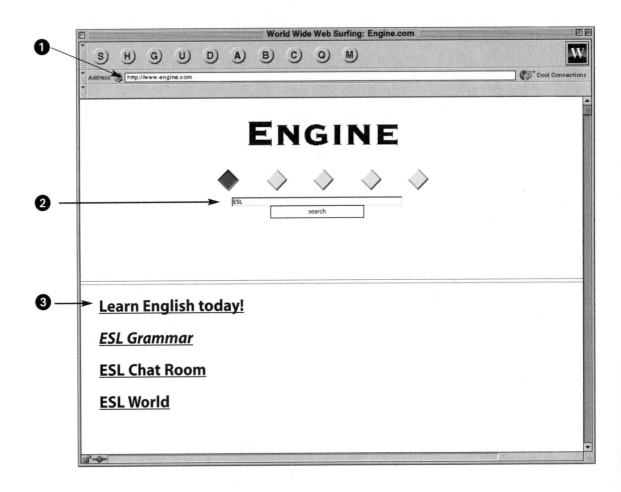

UNIT 2

LANGUAGE AND CULTURE

3

Learning a Second Language

Prereading Preparation

1. Work with a partner. Make a list of things you can do that will help you learn a second language.

Things We Can Do to Help Ourselves Learn a Second Language
1.
2.
3.
4.
5.

2. Compare your list with your other classmates' lists. What can you add to your list?

_____

_____

_____

_____

3. Read the title of this chapter. What will this passage discuss?

_____

Directions: Read each paragraph carefully. Then answer the questions.

Learning a Second Language

Some people learn a second language easily. Other people have trouble learning a new language. How can you help yourself learn a new language, such as English? There are several ways to make learning English a little easier and more interesting.

1. _____ True _____ False   Everyone learns a second language easily.

2. Other people have **trouble** learning a new language. **Trouble** means
   a. difficulty
   b. classes
   c. reasons

3. **Several** means
   a. easier
   b. many
   c. different

4. What do you think the next paragraph will discuss?
   a. problems learning a new language
   b. ways to learn a new language more easily
   c. where to study a second language

> The first step is to feel positive about learning English. If you believe that you can learn, you will learn. Be patient. You do not have to understand everything all at once. It is natural to make mistakes when you learn something new. We can learn from our mistakes. In other words, do not worry about taking risks.

5. What does it mean to feel positive about learning English?
   a. If you believe you can learn, you will learn.
   b. You can understand everything all at once.
   c. You must make mistakes.

6. When you are **patient,** do you worry about learning English very quickly?
   a. Yes
   b. No

7. You do not have to understand everything **all at once.**
   All at once means
   a. slowly
   b. easily
   c. right now

8. We can learn from our mistakes. **In other words,** do not worry about **taking risks.**
   a. What follows **in other words?**
      1. an opposite idea
      2. an example
      3. the same idea
   b. **Taking risks** means
      1. taking chances
      2. working hard
      3. feeling positive

9. What do you think the next paragraph will discuss?
   a. different kinds of languages
   b. making mistakes
   c. the second step

The second step is to practice your English. For example, write in a journal, or diary, every day. You will get used to writing in English, and you will feel comfortable expressing your ideas in English. After several weeks, you will see that your writing is improving. In addition, you must speak English every day. You can practice with your classmates outside class. You will all make mistakes, but gradually you will become comfortable communicating in English.

10. What is a **journal?**
    a. a diary
    b. practice
    c. an example

11. How can you practice your English?
    a. Write in a journal every day.
    b. Practice with your classmates after class.
    c. Both a and b.

12. **After several weeks** means
    a. after a few days
    b. when a few weeks are finished
    c. a week later

13. What follows **in addition?**
    a. more information
    b. the same information
    c. the result

14. **Gradually** means
    a. quickly
    b. carefully
    c. slowly

15. **Communicating** in English means
    a. speaking and listening
    b. reading
    c. studying

16. What will the next paragraph discuss?
    a. making mistakes
    b. feeling comfortable
    c. the third step

The third step is to keep a record of your language learning. You can write this in your journal. After each class, think about what you did. Did you answer a question correctly? Did you understand something the teacher explained? Perhaps the lesson was difficult, but you tried to understand it. Write these accomplishments in your journal.

17. When you **keep a record** of something,
    a. you write it on paper
    b. you remember it
    c. you tell someone

18. ___ True ___ False   You can keep a record of your language learn-ing in your journal.

19. **Perhaps** means
    a. usually
    b. sometimes
    c. maybe

20. **Accomplishments** are
    a. successes
    b. mistakes
    c. lessons

You must be positive about learning English and believe that you can do it. It is important to practice every day and make a record of your achievements. You will enjoy learning English, and you will feel more confidence in yourself.

21. **Achievements** are

    a. accomplishments

    b. lessons

    c. problems

22. Read the following actions. Which ones are accomplishments?

    _____ a. You asked a question in class.

    _____ b. You brought a notebook and a pen to class.

    _____ c. You made a mistake, but you understood why.

    _____ d. You tried to answer a question.

    _____ e. You spoke your native language to a classmate.

Directions: Read the complete passage. When you are finished, you will answer the questions that follow.

Learning a Second Language

1   Some people learn a second language easily. Other people have trouble
2 learning a new language. How can you help yourself learn a new language, such
3 as English? There are several ways to make learning English a little easier and
4 more interesting.
5   The first step is to feel positive about learning English. If you believe that
6 you can learn, you will learn. Be patient. You do not have to understand every-
7 thing all at once. It is natural to make mistakes when you learn something new.
8 We can learn from our mistakes. In other words, do not worry about taking
9 risks.
10   The second step is to practice your English. For example, write in a journal,
11 or diary, every day. You will get used to writing in English, and you will feel com-
12 fortable expressing your ideas in English. After several weeks, you will see that
13 your writing is improving. In addition, you must speak English every day. You
14 can practice with your classmates outside class. You will all make mistakes, but
15 gradually you will become comfortable communicating in English.
16   The third step is to keep a record of your language learning. You can write
17 this in your journal. After each class, think about what you did. Did you answer a
18 question correctly? Did you understand something the teacher explained?
19 Perhaps the lesson was difficult, but you tried to understand it. Write these
20 accomplishments in your journal.
21   You must be positive about learning English and believe that you can do it.
22 It is important to practice every day and make a record of your achievements.
23 You will enjoy learning English, and you will feel more confidence in yourself.

Scanning for Information

Read the following questions. Then go back to the complete passage and scan quickly for the answers. Write them in the space under each question.

1. Are there ways to make learning a second language easier?
   a. Yes
   b. No

2. How many steps are there? _____

3. Describe each step. Then give one example of each step.
   a. _____

      _____

   b. _____

      _____

   c. _____

      _____

4. What is the main idea of this passage?
   a. It is very important to learn a second language.
   b. Some people learn a second language easily. Other people do not.
   c. There are ways to help you learn a second language more easily.

In English, some adjectives (adj.) become adverbs (adv.) by adding the suffix *-ly,* for example, *brief* (adj.), *briefly* (adv.).

Read the following sentences. Decide if the correct word is an adjective or an adverb. Circle your answer. Do the example before you begin.

Example:
a.   John spoke very <u>brief / briefly</u> at the meeting.
          (adj.)   (adv.)

b.   John gave a very <u>brief / briefly</u> speech because he had to leave early.
          (adj.)   (adv.)

1.   This is an <u>easy / easily</u> exercise.
          (adj.)   (adv.)

2.   I can write the answers <u>easy / easily.</u>
          (adj.)   (adv.)

3.   Many people can speak a second language very <u>natural / naturally.</u>
          (adj.)   (adv.)

4.   Children are <u>natural / naturally</u> language learners.
          (adj.)   (adv.)

5.   What is the <u>correct / correctly</u> answer?
          (adj.)   (adv.)

6.   The students answered the question <u>correct / correctly.</u>
          (adj.)   (adv.)

7.   Every day our English <u>gradual / gradually</u> improves.
          (adj.)   (adv.)

8.   This <u>gradual / gradually</u> improvement is exciting.
          (adj.)   (adv.)

Vocabulary in Context

Read the following sentences. Choose the correct word for each sentence. Write your answer in the blank space.

all at once	patient (*adj.*)	risks (*n.*)

1. Alice enjoys trying new, exciting activities. She really likes to take
   _____ .

2. You can't learn how to use a computer _____ . It takes time to
   learn everything you need to know.

3. My mother is a very _____ person. She always takes her time
   and is never in a hurry to finish something.

gradual (*adj.*)	in other words	positive (*adj.*)

4. Clark played the violin every day for four months. He saw a
   _____ improvement in his music.

5. I will take a math test tomorrow. I have studied hard, so I feel very
   _____ about the test.

6. Lucy eats fresh fruit and vegetables every day. She exercises five times a
   week, and she sleeps eight hours a night. _____ , Lucy has a
   very healthy life.

| confidence (*n.*) | in addition | perhaps (*adv.*) | trouble (*n.*) |

7. John is very tired today. _____ he didn't sleep well last night. I'll ask him.

8. We didn't take care of our car. Last week we went on vacation, and we had _____ with our car.

9. Tony needs to have more _____. He is always afraid of doing something wrong.

10. Peter went to the store. He bought milk, meat, bread, and fruit. _____, he got coffee and tea.

Follow-up Activities

1. What is the most difficult part of learning English for you? Talk to several of your classmates. Ask them for suggestions to help you. Talk to several people outside your class. Ask them for suggestions, too. Try some of these suggestions and then report back to your classmates. Tell them which suggestions were the most helpful and explain why.

2. Refer back to your list of things you can do to help yourself learn a language. Work with a partner. Talk about your lists. Decide when you can do these activities, and which language skills each activity will help you develop. Write them in the chart below. There is an example to help you.

Activity	Skill (listening, speaking, reading, writing)	Place I Can Do This Activity
I ask questions when I don't understand.	speaking and listening	in class; in stores; on the street; at a train station or a bus stop; on the telephone

Topics FOR Discussion AND Writing

1. Imagine that you have a friend who plans to come to the United States to study English. Write a letter to your friend. Tell your friend what to expect. Give your friend advice about learning English more easily.

2. Start a journal of your language learning. Use a small notebook that will be easy to carry with you. Write in your journal several times a week. Write about your language-learning accomplishments. In addition, describe the experiences you have with English. For example, when do you use English the most? When is it most difficult to practice English? Describe the ways you try to overcome these difficulties.

Crossword Puzzle

Read the clues on the next page. Write the answers in the correct spaces in the puzzle.

Crossword Puzzle Clues

Across

1. When you study English, be _____ because learning a second language takes time.

3. English _____ many irregular verbs.

5. Is learning English easy? _____, it isn't.

6. We always make _____, or errors, when we learn something new.

7. **She, _____, it**

8. A _____ is a diary.

12. Your _____ are the other students in your class.

13. It takes time to _____ a second language.

14. Keep a _____ of your language in your diary.

15. Class begins at 9 o'clock. If you arrive after 9, you are _____.

16. Keep a diary and write your language learning achievements. This will give you _____.

17. Most students _____ that it is difficult to learn a second language.

Down

1. You need to feel very _____ about learning English. You need to say that you can do it!

2. It is _____, or normal, to make errors when you learn a second language.

4. Your _____, or accomplishments, will help you feel more comfortable.

9. Your pen is _____ your desk.

10. Slowly; after a long time.

11. It is important to _____ English every day.

16. You _____ learn English!

Read the following passage. Fill in each space with the correct word from the list. Use each word only once.

| easily | interesting | learn | such | trouble |

Some people learn a second language _____ (1) . Other people have _____ (2) learning a new language. How can you help yourself _____ (3) a new language, _____ (4) as English? There are several ways to make learning English, a little easier and more _____ (5) .

| achievements | believe | confidence | positive | practice |

You must be _____ (6) about learning English, and you must _____ (7) that you can do it. It is important to _____ (8) every day and make a record of all your _____ (9) . You will enjoy learning English, and you will feel more _____ (10) in yourself.

4

Food and Culture

Prereading Preparation

1. What kind of food do you like to eat? For example, do you like American food, Korean food, Mexican food, etc.?

2. Does everyone like to eat the same food? Why or why not?

3. Work together with your classmates in small groups. Talk about food. First, write each student's name and country below. What food does each student prefer? Give examples of the kinds of food each student likes. Write your answers below.

Name	Country	Example of Food

4. Look at your list. What do you notice about the types of food each student likes?

5. With your group, write a definition, or explanation, of **culture.** Write your definition on the blackboard. Compare it with your classmates' definitions. What does **culture** mean?

6. The title of this article is "Food and Culture." What do you think this reading will discuss?

_____ a. All people like to eat the same kinds of food.

_____ b. Most people like to eat food from their own culture.

_____ c. Most people like to eat food from other cultures.

_____ d. Everyone thinks that the same kinds of food are good to eat.

_____ e. Not everyone thinks that the same kinds of food are good to eat.

_____ f. We all like some kinds of food because we always eat these kinds of food.

_____ g. We don't like some kinds of food because they are strange to us.

Directions: Read each paragraph carefully. Then answer the questions.

Food and Culture

What kind of food do you like to eat? Do you eat raw fish? Dog meat? Cheese? Many people prefer to eat food from their own culture. In other words, they like to eat food that they are familiar with.

Some people dislike certain food because they are not accustomed to it. The Japanese enjoy eating raw horse meat, but few Americans would want to taste it. Many Asians strongly dislike pizza, which is a very popular food in the United States. Milk is a very common drink in the United States for all people, young and old. In contrast, only babies drink milk in China.

1. Many people prefer to eat food from their own culture. **In other words, they like to eat food that they are familiar with.**

   a. These two sentences

      1. have opposite meanings

      2. have the same meanings

      3. are examples of each other

   b. **In other words**

      1. explains the first sentence

      2. gives an example

      3. shows a contrast

2. When a person is **accustomed to** something, it means that
   a. the person is familiar with it
   b. the person eats it
   c. the person dislikes it

3. The Japanese probably enjoy eating horse meat because
   a. it tastes good
   b. they are accustomed to it
   c. they dislike certain foods

4. **Few** Americans would want to **taste** raw horse meat.
   a. **Few** Americans are
      1. many
      2. some
      3. not many
   b. In this sentence, **taste** means
      1. delicious
      2. flavor
      3. try

5. _____ True _____ False   Many Americans dislike pizza.

6. _____ True _____ False   Only babies drink milk in the United States.

7. **Strongly** means
   a. really
   b. sometimes
   c. carefully

8. **In contrast** shows
   a. a similarity
   b. an example
   c. a difference

Some people do not eat particular food for religious reasons. For instance, Hindus do not eat beef because cows are considered sacred. Jewish people and Moslems do not eat pork because pigs are thought to be unclean.

Sociologists say that people prefer the food that they grew up with. As a cultural group, we learn to like what is available to us. This is why in Africa some people eat termites, in Asia some people eat dog meat, and in Europe some people eat blood sausages.

9. **For instance** means
   a. because
   b. as a result
   c. for example

10. _____ True _____ False   Hindus do not eat beef for religious reasons.

11. Why don't Jewish people and Moslems eat pork?
   a. They don't like it.
   b. They believe that pigs are unclean.
   c. They do not have pigs in their countries.

12. What do you think a **sociologist** is?

   _____

13. **We learn to like what is available to us.** What are some examples from the reading?
   a. _____
   b. _____
   c. _____

14. What do you think a **cultural group** is?

   _____

Sometimes we need to change our eating habits. If we move or travel to a new place with a different culture, our favorite meat, fruit, and vegetables may not be available to us. As a result, we have to eat food that is different from the food we are used to. Slowly, this strange food becomes familiar to us. Our tastes change, and we begin to enjoy eating the food that used to seem unusual to us.

15. Why might we need to change our eating habits?

_____

_____

16. _____ True _____ False   When we eat food that is new to us, we may slowly become accustomed to it.

17. _____ True _____ False   We are never able to enjoy unusual food.

18. **Slowly** means
    a. gradually
    b. correctly
    c. quickly

19. **Our tastes change.** In this sentence, **tastes** means
    a. delicious
    b. preferences
    c. try

Directions: Read the complete passage. When you are finished, answer the questions that follow.

Food and Culture

1   What kind of food do you like to eat? Do you eat raw fish? Dog meat?
2 Cheese? Many people prefer to eat food from their own culture. In other words,
3 they like to eat food that they are familiar with.
4   Some people dislike certain food because they are not accustomed to it. The
5 Japanese enjoy eating raw horse meat, but few Americans would want to taste it.
6 Many Asians strongly dislike pizza, which is a popular food in the United States.
7 Milk is a very common drink in the United States for all people, young and old.
8 In contrast, only babies drink milk in China.
9   Some people do not eat particular food for religious reasons. For instance,
10 Hindus do not eat beef because cows are considered sacred. Jewish people and
11 Moslems do not eat pork because pigs are thought to be unclean.
12   Sociologists say that people prefer the food that they grew up with. As a
13 cultural group, we learn to like what is available to us. This is why in Africa

some people eat termites, in Asia some people eat dog meat, and in Europe some people eat blood sausages.

Sometimes we need to change our eating habits. If we move or travel to a new place with a different culture, our favorite meat, fruit, and vegetables may not be available to us. As a result, we have to eat food that is different from the food we are used to. Slowly, this strange food becomes familiar to us. Our tastes change, and we begin to enjoy eating the food that used to seem unusual to us.

Read the following questions. Then go back to the complete passage and scan quickly for the answers. Write them in the space under each question.

1. What kind of food do most people like to eat?

    _____

2. Why do people dislike certain food?

    _____

3. What are some examples of religious reasons why people do not eat certain food?

    _____

    _____

4. In Africa some people eat termites, in Asia some people eat dog meat, and in Europe some people eat blood sausages. Why?

    _____

5. What is the main idea of this passage?
    a. The food we like is a result of our cultural group.
    b. Asian people strongly dislike pizza.
    c. It is possible to change our eating habits.

Word Forms

In English, some words can be either nouns (n.) or verbs (v.), for example, *light*. Read the following sentences. Decide if the word is a noun or a verb. Circle your answer. Do the example below before you begin.

Example:
   a. Bob has many bright <u>lights</u> in his house.
                (n. or v.)

   b. Bob always <u>lights</u> them when he gets home in the evening.
                (n. or v.)

1. I enjoy the different <u>tastes</u> of fresh fruit.
                (n. or v.)

2. Fruit always <u>tastes</u> delicious to me.
                (n. or v.)

3. Carmen <u>moved</u> to California last summer.
                (n. or v.)

4. It was an exciting <u>move</u>.
                (n. or v.)

5. I'm very thirsty. May I have a cold <u>drink</u>?
                (n. or v.)

6. I always <u>drink</u> water when I am thirsty.
                (n. or v.)

7. Every semester the students <u>change</u> their class.
                (n. or v.)

8. This <u>change</u> is very interesting for them.
                (n. or v.)

Read the following sentences. Choose the correct word for each sentence. Write your answer in the blank space.

for instance	in contrast	popular (*adj.*)

1. Steven loves all kinds of fruit. _____, he enjoys apples, bananas, and grapes.

2. Ice cream is a _____ dessert. Many people eat it.

3. I don't eat eggs. _____, my sister eats an egg for break-fast every day.

common (*adj.*)	few (*adj.*)	in other words	prefers (*v.*)

4. Kim _____ to eat Korean food. She doesn't really like American food.

5. Luis comes to class every day, always does his homework, and studies hard. _____, Luis is a very good student.

6. Cereal is a _____ breakfast food in the United States. Many Americans eat it every day.

7. Milk is usually for children in China. _____ adults drink milk there.

accustomed to (*v.*)	strongly (*adv.*)	unusual (*adj.*)

8. When I first came to the United States, I did not like American food. Now I am _____ it. I enjoy American food.

9. Raw horse meat is an _____ food in the United States. Almost no one eats it.

10. Murat _____ dislikes Mexican food. He thinks it tastes too spicy.

Follow-up Activities

1. This chapter talks about food and culture. It also tells us that sometimes our taste, or preference, for food can change. Is your taste in food now different from your taste in the past? What different food do you want to try in the future? Work with three partners. Discuss your ideas and write them below.

Food I Liked in the Past	Food I Like Now	Food I Want to Try in the Future
1.	1.	1.
2.	2.	2.
3.	3.	3.
4.	4.	4.

2. As a class, combine your lists of food you like now and food you want to try in the future. Which type of food is the most popular among your classmates? Which type of food do most of your classmates want to try in the future? In your city, where can you go to try these different types of food?

3. Alone, or with your classmates, go to a restaurant that serves a kind of food you have never eaten before. Eat lunch or dinner there. Discuss the food with your classmates. Report back to your class. Describe the food you ate and why you liked it or didn't like it.

Topics FOR *Discussion* AND *Writing*

1. Go to a supermarket. Write a paragraph about the supermarket. How is it similar to food stores in your country? How is it different? Share your paragraph with your classmates. What did you notice that your class-mates didn't? What did your classmates observe that you didn't?

2. Write in your journal. Describe your experience eating food from a differ-ent culture. Was it a positive experience? Why or why not? Share your experience with your classmates. Whose experience is the most interesting?

F.　Crossword Puzzle

Read the clues on the next page. Write the answers in the correct spaces in the puzzle.

Crossword Puzzle Clues

Across

3. It is _____, or usual, for different people to like different kinds of food.

4. Americans usually eat three times a day: at breakfast, at _____, and at dinner.

7. Some people _____ dislike certain food and will not eat it.

10. What kind _____ food do people eat in your country?

13. There are many _____ why people do not eat certain food.

14. We become _____ to certain food because we grow up eating it.

15. We all _____ kinds of food that we like and don't like.

17. The food we like to eat depends on the _____ and the country we live in.

18. When we _____ to another country, we learn about different kinds of food.

19. Beef is not acceptable _____ for Hindus.

21. When we have to eat food that is different, we _____ become accustomed to it. It takes time.

23. We like to eat what we _____ used to eating.

24. Many people eat the food that is _____ to them. It is easy to get.

25. Most people _____ the food from their own culture and enjoy eating it.

Down

1. Sometimes people do _____ like food that looks or smells different.

2. Pizza is very _____ in the United States. Most people like it.

5. In China, it is very _____ for adults to drink milk. Only babies drink milk there.

6. When we _____ our eating habits, we learn to like different kinds of foods.

8. Some people do not like the _____ of certain food, even when it looks and smells good.

9. In every culture, people eat certain kinds of food _____ special holidays.

11. We usually like food that is _____ to us. We like food that we are used to.

12. Some people do not eat certain food for _____ reasons.

16. We _____ to eat food we are used to. We want to eat food we are accustomed to.

17. In Asia, some people eat dog meat. In _____, in the United States, no one eats dog meat.

20. The food that some people enjoy eating, other people _____ very much.

22. Is there any food that most people like to eat? _____, there is.

24. Each; every

Cloze Quiz

Read the following passages. Fill in each space with the correct word from the list. Use each word only once.

accustomed	contrast	drink	popular	taste

Some people dislike a certain food because they are not

_____ to it. The Japanese enjoy eating raw horse meat, but few
(1)

Americans would want to _____ it. Many Asians strongly dislike
(2)

pizza, which is a very _____ food in the United States. Milk is a
(3)

very common _____ in the United States for all people, young
(4)

and old. In _____, only babies drink milk in China.
(5)

different	enjoy	familiar	habits	result

Sometimes we need to change our eating _____. If we
(6)

move or travel to a new place with a _____ culture, our favorite
(7)

meat, fruit, and vegetables may not be available to us. As a

_____, we have to eat food that is different from the food we are
(8)

used to. Slowly, this strange food becomes _____ to us. Our
(9)

tastes change, and we begin to _____ eating the food that used
(10)

to seem unusual to us.

1. Many teenagers and young adults in Asia now enjoy Western-style or American food. Do you think this diet will change their health? How?

2. Read the questions. Then watch the video and answer them.
   a. What kind of food does Mr. Hirobayashi eat?
   b. What kind of food does Akiko Hirobayashi like?
   c. Does the doctor feel good about the changes in Japanese food?
   d. How is Western food changing the health and the looks of Japanese people?

3. The Hirobayashis have a young daughter. What kind of food do you think she will eat in the future?

Surfing THE INTERNET

Go to the Internet and enter the address for a search engine such as **google.com, msn.com,** or **yahoo.com.** Enter the search word for your favorite food or recipe. For example, you might look up *hamburger recipe.* Choose a good recipe and tell your classmates about it.

Optional Activity: Find out about food from another culture. Go to the Internet and enter the search words *food* and then the name of another country. Read the recipe and learn the new vocabulary. Tell a partner or your class if the food sounds good.

UNIT 3

EXERCISE AND FITNESS

5

The Importance of Exercise for Children

Prereading Preparation

1. Look at the picture. What are the children doing?

2. Work with a partner from another country. Discuss the questions in the information chart and fill in the answers.

What country are you from?	Do children exercise in school?	How often do children exercise in school?	What kinds of exercise do the children do?
1.			
2.			

3. Read the title of this passage. What do you think the reading will discuss?

Directions: Read each paragraph carefully. Then answer the questions.

The Importance of Exercise for Children

Joseph is a very busy 8-year-old boy. In the fall, he plays on a roller hockey team. He practices every Tuesday and Thursday afternoon and has a roller hockey game every Sunday morning. In the winter, Joseph plays basketball. His team practices one evening a week. They have a basketball game every Saturday morning. In the spring and summer, Joseph plays baseball. His team has a game twice a week and practices at least once. It is easy to see that Joseph is very active <u>after</u> school.

1. Why is Joseph **a very busy 8-year-old boy?**
   a. He goes to school a lot.
   b. He plays many different sports.
   c. He plays on a roller hockey team.

2. **His team practices one evening a week.** This means
   a. every night during the week
   b. at 1:00 during the week
   c. one night every week

3. Why is **after** underlined?
   a. for emphasis
   b. because it is a new word
   c. to show a contrast

4. What do you think the next paragraph will discuss?

   _____

In contrast, while most American children are <u>in</u> school, they have a physical education class just once a week for 45 minutes. Boys and girls from kindergarten to grade 12 do not have to have a physical education class in school every day. They do not have to exercise.

Not all American children are as active in sports after school as Joseph is. Therefore, these boys and girls need to exercise in school. Many people believe that the fitness and health of American children are in trouble. In fact, 40 percent of children age 5 to 8 may be unhealthy already. For example, many have high blood pressure, are overweight, or have high cholesterol. Doctors believe that these conditions are the result of physical inactivity and poor diet.

5. **In contrast** shows
   a. an example
   b. a similarity
   c. a difference

6. What is a **physical education class?**
   a. a science class
   b. an exercise class
   c. an outdoor class

7. How often do most American children exercise in school?

   _____

8. _____ True _____ False   Most schoolchildren have a physical education class every day in the United States.

9. Not all American children are as active in sports after school as Joseph is. **Therefore,** these boys and girls need to exercise in school.
   a. The first sentence means that most American children
      1. are also very active in sports, like Joseph
      2. are more active in sports than Joseph is
      3. are less active in sports than Joseph is
   b. **Therefore** means
      1. also
      2. as a result
      3. for example

10. Many people believe that the **fitness** and health of American children are in trouble.

    a. **Fitness** means

        1. good physical condition

        2. exercise

        3. sports

    b. Many people believe that the fitness and health of American children

        1. are in America

        2. are interesting

        3. are a problem

11. _____ True _____ False   Many American children may be unhealthy already.

12. Doctors believe that these conditions are the result of **physical inactivity** and poor diet.

    What is **physical inactivity?**

    a. sports

    b. no exercise

    c. high blood pressure

In many countries in the world, all schoolchildren have to do one hour of exercise every day. These exercises do not have to be team sports. They may be simple, such as running, jumping, or climbing ropes. Doctors believe that habits learned early are more likely to stay with us through life. School is the perfect place to learn these habits, or practices. Active, healthy children who exercise regularly can become active, healthy adults.

13. _____ True _____ False   Running, jumping, and climbing ropes are always team sports.

14. Doctors believe that **habits** learned early are more likely to **stay with us through life.** School is the perfect place to learn these habits, or practices.

    a. **Habits** are
       1. places
       2. sports
       3. practices

    b. What kinds of **habits** are these?
       1. reading habits
       2. exercise habits
       3. study habits

    c. **Stay with us through life** means
       1. we will continue to do it
       2. we will start these habits early
       3. we will not change

15. _____ True _____ False   The author believes that American children need to exercise in school more often.

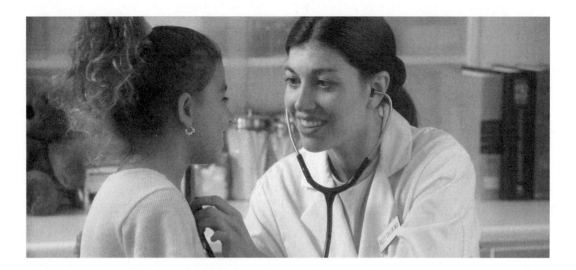

Directions: Read the complete passage. When you are finished, you will answer the questions that follow.

The Importance of Exercise for Children

1   Joseph is a very busy 8-year-old boy. In the fall, he plays on a roller hockey
2   team. He practices every Tuesday and Thursday afternoon and has a roller
3   hockey game every Sunday morning. In the winter, Joseph plays basketball. His
4   team practices one evening a week. They have a basketball game every Saturday
5   morning. In the spring and summer, Joseph plays baseball. His team has a game
6   twice a week and practices at least once. It is easy to see that Joseph is very
7   active <u>after</u> school.

8   In contrast, while most American children are <u>in</u> school, they have a physi-
9   cal education class just once a week for 45 minutes. Boys and girls from kinder-
10 garten to grade 12 do not have to have a physical education class in school every
11 day. They do not have to exercise.

12 Not all American children are as active in sports after school as Joseph is.
13 Therefore, these boys and girls need to exercise in school. Many people believe
14 that the fitness and health of American children are in trouble. In fact, 40 per-
15 cent of children age 5 to 8 may be unhealthy already. For example, many have
16 high blood pressure, are overweight, or have high cholesterol. Doctors believe
17 that these conditions are the result of physical inactivity and poor diet.

18 In many countries in the world, all schoolchildren have to do one hour of
19 exercise every day. These exercises do not have to be team sports. They may be
20 simple, such as running, jumping, or climbing ropes. Doctors believe that habits
21 learned early are more likely to stay with us through life. School is the perfect
22 place to learn these habits, or practices. Active, healthy children who exercise
23 regularly can become active, healthy adults.

Read the following questions. Then go back to the complete passage and scan quickly for the answers. Write them in the space under each question.

1. What sports does Joseph play after school?

   _____

   _____

2. How often do most American children exercise <u>in</u> school?

   _____

   _____

3. a. Is physical activity important for children? _____

   b. What can happen when children do not exercise?

   _____

4. Active, healthy children who exercise regularly can become active, healthy adults. Why?
   a. because they were healthy children
   b. because they practiced many sports
   c. because they will continue their healthy habits

5. What is the main idea of this passage?
   a. Joseph does not exercise in school.
   b. Schoolchildren around the world exercise every day.
   c. It is very important for children to exercise in school.

In English, some words can be either nouns (n.) or verbs (v.), for example, *drink*.

Read the following sentences. Decide if the word is a noun or a verb. Circle your answer. Do the example before you begin.

Example:
a. I always <u>drink</u> water when I exercise.
      (n. or v.)

b. This <u>drink</u> is very cold.
      (n. or v.)

1. Liz <u>practices</u> the piano for one hour every day.
      (n. or v.)

2. Piano <u>practice</u> is fun for her.
      (n. or v.)

3. <u>Exercise</u> is important to our health.
    (n. or v.)

4. We <u>exercise</u> every afternoon.
      (n. or v.)

5. I sometimes <u>diet</u> to lose weight.
          (n. or v.)

6. My <u>diet</u> includes a lot of fruit and vegetables.
      (n. or v.)

7. Tom made many <u>changes</u> in his lifestyle.
          (n. or v.)

8. Tom also <u>changed</u> his eating habits.
          (n. or v.)

Vocabulary in Context

Read the following sentences. Choose the correct answer for each sentence. Write your answer in the blank space.

at least	habit (*n.*)	in contrast

1. I try to eat _____ two pieces of fruit every day. I always eat an apple and a banana. Sometimes I eat an orange, too.

2. It is a good _____ to exercise three times a week. I usually exercise on Mondays, Thursdays, and Saturdays.

3. Eric doesn't enjoy team sports. _____, his brother Kyle plays basketball, baseball, and roller hockey.

active (*adj.*)	as a result	practice (*v.*)	regularly (*adv.*)

4. Many adults exercise _____. For example, some people run every morning before work.

5. Many children don't exercise every day. _____, some children are overweight.

6. Joseph is a very _____ child. He exercises all the time and plays many kinds of sports.

7. If you want to be a good swimmer, you must _____. You must swim several times a week.

therefore	condition (*n.*)	likely (*adj.*)

8. Some children are overweight. This _____ is sometimes a result of a poor diet.

9. Lynn's doctor told her to lose weight. _____, she is trying to eat less and exercise more.

10. Children who exercise are very _____ to grow up and continue to exercise as adults.

1. Refer to all the physical activities you and your classmates listed at the beginning of this chapter. Put these activities into the appropriate categories of **sports, exercises,** and **martial arts** in the chart below. Some activities may belong in more than one category. For example, swimming can be a sport or an exercise.

Martial Arts	Sports	Exercises
	swimming	swimming

2. Imagine that a friend has asked you to give suggestions for activities that children can do in order to get exercise. Work with two or three class-mates. Make a list of 10 ways that children can get exercise that would be fun for them. When you are finished, write your suggestions on the black-board. As a class, decide which 10 activities children will enjoy the most.

Topics FOR *Discussion* AND *Writing*

1. Refer back to the second follow-up activity. Write a letter to your friend and describe your 10 recommendations.

2. Write in your journal. Describe the most exciting sports event you have ever watched or participated in. What was the event? What happened? Why was it exciting for you?

Crossword Puzzle

Read the clues on the next page. Write the answers in the correct spaces in the puzzle.

Crossword Puzzle Clues

Across

1. Joseph _____ roller hockey games on Sunday mornings.

2. Joseph is physically active, _____ many children are not.

3. Soccer, basketball, and baseball are _____.

5. Soccer and baseball _____ outdoor sports.

7. Children _____ exercise to be healthy.

8. Some children have a poor _____. This means that they do not eat healthy food.

10. Exercise can be _____. It can be enjoyable.

12. When children sit too much, they do not get enough _____ activity.

15. Joseph needs to exercise all his _____, not just while he is a child.

17. A team needs to _____ every week.

18. Joseph is a very _____ boy. He plays on many teams after school.

19. Some children are very _____ with sports. They play after school and on weekends, too.

Down

1. Regular exercise and a healthy diet are good _____ that we need all our lives.

3. **He, _____, it.**

4. A person who is heavy, or fat, is _____.

6. Everyone needs to exercise _____. We need to exercise every week.

9. Children can do all kinds of _____, for example, running, jumping, or climbing rope.

11. Some conditions, such as being overweight, can be _____.

13. Joseph exercises every day. In _____, some children do not exercise at all.

14. Physical _____ means being in good physical condition.

16. We can do some sports alone, for example, running. We do other sports with a _____.

G. Cloze Quiz

Read the following paragraphs. Fill in each space with the correct word from the list. Use each word only once.

busy	every	practices	winter
easy	morning	week	

Joseph is a very _____ 8-year-old boy. In the fall, he plays
                  (1)

on a roller hockey team. He _____ every Tuesday and Thursday
                  (2)

afternoon and has a roller hockey game every Sunday _____. In
                  (3)

the _____, Joseph plays basketball. His team has a basketball
    (4)

game _____ Saturday morning. In the spring and summer,
      (5)

Joseph plays baseball. His team has a game twice a _____ and
              (6)

practices often. It is _____ to see that Joseph is very active after
      (7)

school.

active	exercise	result	trouble
believe	overweight	therefore	unhealthy

Not all American children are as _____ in sports after school
             (8)

as Joseph is. _____, these boys and girls need to
      (9)

_____ in school. Many people believe that the fitness and
  (10)

health of American children are in _____. In fact, 40 percent of
         (11)

children age 5 to 8 may be _____ already. For example, many
        (12)

have high blood pressure, are _____, or have high cholesterol.
        (13)

Doctors _____ that these conditions are the _____
    (14)   (15)

of physical inactivity and poor diet.

6

The New York City Marathon: A World Race

Prereading Preparation

1. Look at the picture. How many people do you think are running in this marathon?

2. Read the title of this chapter. Why is the New York City Marathon a world race? Where is this race? Who runs in this race?

3. Work with two or three classmates. What are some reasons why people run in marathons? Make a list. Compare your list with your classmates' lists.

Directions: Read each paragraph carefully. Then answer the questions.

The New York City Marathon: A World Race

The New York City Marathon was started by a man named Fred Lebow. It began in 1970 as a small, unimportant race. Only 127 people ran, and just 55 of them finished. They ran around Central Park four times. Few people watched them run. However, over the years, the marathon grew and became more popular.

Today, people come from all over the world to run in the marathon. Runners must be at least 18 years old, but there is no age limit. In fact, the oldest runner was an 89-year-old man. Recently, more than 27,000 people ran in the New York City Marathon. Large crowds cheered the runners and offered the participants cold drinks and encouragement.

1. Only 127 people ran, and **just** 55 of them finished.
   Just means
   a. because
   b. only
   c. more than

2. ____ True ____ False   All 127 people finished the first marathon.

3. **Over the years** means
   a. as the years went by
   b. one year after
   c. many more years

4. ____ True ____ False   Runners cannot be younger than 18 years old.

5. **There is no age limit** means
   a. people of any age can run
   b. older people cannot run
   c. anyone older than 18 years old can run

The course of the marathon has changed, too. Instead of running around Central Park, the participants go through the five boroughs of New York City: Queens, Brooklyn, Manhattan, the Bronx, and Staten Island. The marathon begins at the base of the Verrazano Narrows Bridge in Staten Island. The runners go across the bridge into Brooklyn. Then they go up through Queens and into the Bronx. The marathon finishes in Central Park in Manhattan. The complete course is 26 miles, 385 yards, and takes the best runners less than 3 hours.

6. The **course** of the marathon has changed, too. In this sentence, **course** means
   a. direction
   b. class
   c. reason

7. The **participants** are
   a. the crowd
   b. the runners
   c. the organizers

8. _____ True _____ False   The fastest runners can finish the race in 3 hours or more.

Although it has changed since 1970, the New York City Marathon is always exciting. Through the years, many unusual events have happened during the marathon. For example, Pat Tuz and John Weilbaker got married a few minutes before the race. Then, they ran the race with their wedding party. Some people run the whole marathon as a family. Other people run the race backwards.

In the fall of 1992, Fred Lebow, the founder of the New York City Marathon, slowly ran his last race. He was very ill with cancer, but he did not want to stop running. In October 1994, Fred died. However, the New York City Marathon, and all its excitement, will continue for many years to come.

9. _____ True _____ False   Pat Tuz and John Weilbaker ran the marathon backwards.

10. _____ True _____ False   Fred Lebow ran his last race in 1994.

11. **In the fall** means
    a. when someone fell down
    b. the time before winter
    c. the beginning of the year

New York City Marathon Route
(total distance 26.2 miles)

Bronx

Central Park

20 Miles

Queens

15 Miles

Finish

Queensboro Bridge

Manhattan

10 Miles

5 Miles

Brooklyn

Staten Island

Start

Verrazano Narrows Bridge

N
S

Directions: Now read the complete passage. When you are finished, you will answer the questions that follow.

The New York City Marathon: A World Race

1   The New York City Marathon was started by a man named Fred Lebow. It
2 began in 1970 as a small, unimportant race. Only 127 people ran, and just 55 of
3 them finished. They ran around Central Park four times. Few people watched
4 them run. However, over the years, the marathon grew and became more
5 popular.

6   Today, people come from all over the world to run in the marathon. Runners
7 must be at least 18 years old, but there is no age limit. In fact, the oldest runner
8 was an 89-year-old man. Recently, more than 27,000 people ran in the New York
9 City Marathon. Large crowds cheered the runners and offered the participants
10 cold drinks and encouragement.

11   The course of the marathon has changed, too. Instead of running around
12 Central Park, the participants go through the five boroughs of New York City:
13 Queens, Brooklyn, Manhattan, the Bronx, and Staten Island. The marathon
14 begins at the base of the Verrazano Narrows Bridge in Staten Island. The runners
15 go across the bridge into Brooklyn. Then they go up through Queens and into the
16 Bronx. The marathon finishes in Central Park in Manhattan. The complete
17 course is 26 miles, 385 yards, and takes the best runners less than 3 hours.

18   Although it has changed since 1970, the New York City Marathon is always
19 exciting. Through the years, many unusual events have happened during the
20 marathon. For example, Pat Tuz and John Weilbaker got married a few minutes
21 before the race. Then, they ran the race with their wedding party. Some people
22 run the whole marathon as a family. Other people run the race backwards.

23   In the fall of 1992, Fred Lebow, the founder of the New York City Marathon,
24 slowly ran his last race. He was very ill with cancer, but he did not want to stop
25 running. In October 1994, Fred died. However, the New York City Marathon, and
26 all its excitement, will continue for many years to come.

A. Scanning for Information

Read the following questions. Then go back to the complete passage and scan quickly for the answers. Write them in the space under each question.

1. Describe two ways that the New York City Marathon has changed.

    a. _____

    b. _____

2. What do the crowds do during the marathon?

    _____

    _____

3. What are some unusual events that have happened during the marathon?

    _____

    _____

4. What is the main idea of this passage?
    a. The New York City Marathon began in 1970.
    b. The founder of the New York City Marathon was an important man.
    c. The New York City Marathon is a very popular and exciting race.

B. Word Forms

In English, some verbs (v.) can become nouns (n.) by adding the suffix *-ment,* for example, *agree* (v.), *agreement* (n.). Read the following sentences. Decide if the correct word is a noun or a verb. Circle your answer. Do the example before you begin.

Example:

    a. My wife and I <u>agree / agreement</u> that we must both take care of our
                     (v.)   (n.)
        children.

    b. This <u>agree / agreement</u> is very important to us.
           (v.)   (n.)

1. The crowds <u>excite / excitement</u> the runners in the marathon.
            (v.)   (n.)

2. There is a lot of <u>excite / excitement</u> all day.
               (v.)   (n.)

3. Many people <u>encourage / encouragement</u> the runners by cheering for them.
             (v.)   (n.)

4. The crowds' <u>encourage / encouragement</u> is very important to the runners.
            (v.)   (n.)

5. Andy has made a lot of <u>improve / improvement</u> in his English this semester.
              (v.)   (n.)

6. Every day Andy's English <u>improves / improvement</u> a little more.
               (v.)   (n.)

7. English is a <u>require / requirement</u> in all American universities.
            (v.)   (n.)

8. All American universities also <u>require / requirement</u> a high school degree
                (v.)   (n.)
        for all students.

Vocabulary in Context

Read the following sentences. Choose the correct answer for each sentence. Write your answer in the blank space.

| cheer (*v.*)   encouragement (*n.*)   instead of |

1. The crowds _____ when they watch baseball games.

2. I want to go swimming, but it is raining. _____ going to the beach, I will go to the swimming pool at the college.

3. My parents always believed I could succeed. Their _____ helped me to do well in school.

| course (*n.*)   just (*adv.*)   limit (*n.*)   popular (*adj.*) |

4. Marathons are very _____ in American cities.

5. The speed _____ on this highway is 55 miles an hour. You cannot drive faster than 55.

6. The _____ for horse races is usually dirt, but sometimes it is grass.

7. I am taking _____ one class this semester because I have a job. I don't have time to take more than one class.

| however   participant (*n.*)   unusual (*adj.*) |

8. Snow is _____ in New York City in April. It very rarely happens.

9. Robert wants to be a _____ in the next New York City Marathon. He runs 25 miles every week to prepare himself.

10. It is usually very cold in January. _____, this year it was very mild.

1. The following chart shows the number of participants in the New York City Marathon from 1970 through 1994. Look at it carefully, and then answer the questions that follow.

NEW YORK CITY MARATHON—NUMBER OF RUNNERS

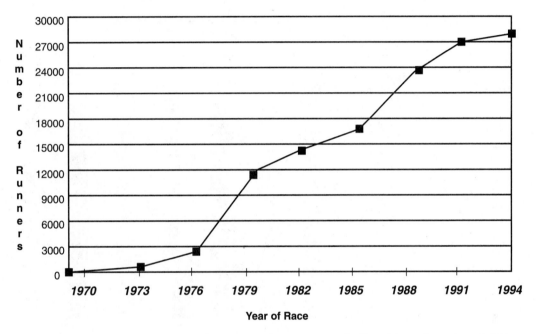

a. More than 3,000 people ran in the New York City Marathon in 1976.

   1. Yes

   2. No

b. More than 18,000 people ran in the New York City Marathon in 1985.

   1. Yes

   2. No

c. More than 27,000 people ran in the New York City Marathon in 1991.

   1. Yes

   2. No

d. More than 27,000 people ran in the New York City Marathon in 1994.

   1. Yes

   2. No

e. The largest increase in the number of runners occurred from 1976 to 1979.
1. Yes
2. No

2. The following chart shows the finishing times of the men and women participants in the New York City Marathon from 1970 through 1994. Look at it carefully. Then read the sentences that follow. Fill in the blank with the word **women** or **men** to make the sentence correct.

NEW YORK CITY MARATHON—WINNING TIMES

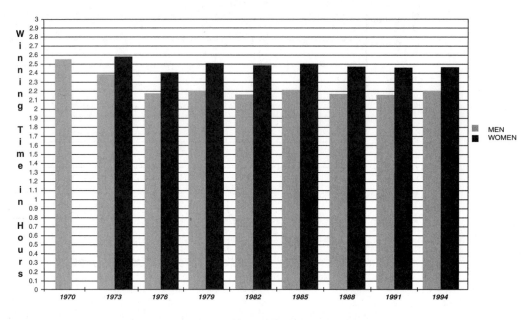

Year of Race

Look at the chart above.
a. In 1970 only _____ ran in the Marathon.
b. In 1985 the winning time for _____ was 2.2 hours.
c. In 1979 the winning time for _____ was 2.5 hours.
d. In 1994 the winning time for _____ was 2.2 hours.

Topics FOR *Discussion* AND *Writing*

1. Work with two or three classmates. Have you or your partners ever run in a marathon? How did you prepare for it? What was the race like? If you haven't run in a marathon, do you want to? Why or why not?

2. Imagine that your friend wants to run in a marathon. In your group, discuss some advice that you can give your friend. Compare your suggestions with your other classmates' suggestions. Which suggestions are the best? Write a letter to your friend and give him or her your advice.

3. Write in your journal. Describe a popular sports event in your country. What is the event? Who participates? Why do people enjoy watching it?

Crossword Puzzle

Read the clues on the next page. Write the answers in the correct spaces in the puzzle.

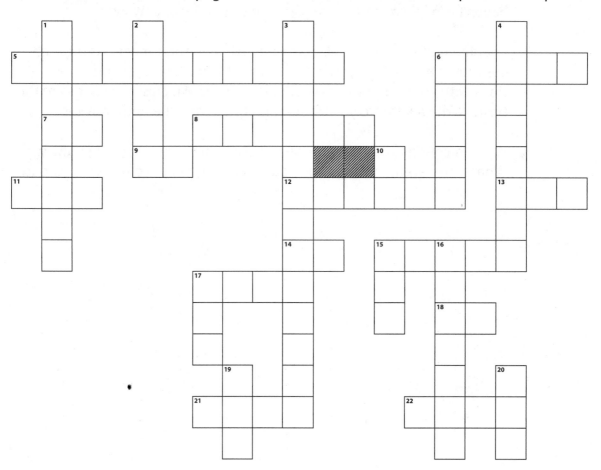

Crossword Puzzle Clues

Across

5. Each _____ in the race gets a number for identification.

6. A huge _____ of people lines the route of the race in order to watch.

7. The race begins _____ the base of the Verrazano Narrows Bridge.

8. Everyone runs _____ the bridge from Staten Island to Brooklyn.

9. Many people want _____ run in the New York City race.

11. **He, _____, it**

12. Every _____ has trained for many months.

13. At the end of the race, all the athletes _____ a medal.

14. People from all over the world _____ to New York to be in the race.

15. The _____ of the race runs through all the boroughs of New York City.

17. The _____ is about 26 miles in length.

18. **I, me; we, _____.**

21. In the first race, _____ half the people finished.

22. The race is always held in the _____, when the weather is cool.

Down

1. A _____ is a 26-mile race.

2. There is no age _____ for the race. Some very old people have run in this race.

3. The people who watch the race offer _____ to the runners.

4. Brooklyn, Queens, Manhattan, Staten Island, and the Bronx are the five _____ of New York City.

6. The people who watch the race _____ as the runners pass them on the route.

10. The race is always held _____ Sunday.

15. Thousands of people run in the race, but not everyone _____ finish it.

16. Sometimes people do _____, or strange, things during the race.

17. Most people _____ in the race, but some people simply walk fast.

19. Only a few people win the race, _____ everyone feels successful.

20. Each; every

Cloze Quiz

Read the following paragraphs. Fill in each space with the correct word from the list.
Use each word only once.

cheered	limit	oldest	recently
encouragement	marathon	participants	

Today people come from all over the world to run in the

_____. Runners must be at least 18 years old, but there is no age
       (1)

_____. In fact, the _____ runner was an 89-year-old
       (2)   (3)

man. _____, more than 27,000 people ran in the New York City
       (4)

Marathon. Large crowds _____ the runners and offered the
                              (5)

_____ cold drinks and _____.
       (6)   (7)

backwards	example	race	since
events	exciting	ran	whole

Although it has changed _____ 1970, the New York City
                              (8)

Marathon is always _____. Through the years, many unusual
                        (9)

_____ have happened during the marathon. For
       (10)

_____, Pat Tuz and John Weilbaker got married a few minutes
       (11)

before the _____. Then they _____ the race with
             (12)   (13)

their wedding party. Some people run the _____ marathon as a
                                              (14)

family. Other people run the race _____.
                                        (15)

1. Do you think most children in the United States have good health? What problems do some children have? What can they do to improve their health?

2. Read the true/false questions. Then watch the video and answer them.

   a. Children in the United States have less health insurance than they used to have. _____ T _____ F

   b. According to the video, 82% of children in the United States have good or excellent health. _____ T _____ F

   c. Some of the news about children is bad. _____ T _____ F

   d. Children's diets don't have enough fat. _____ T _____ F

   e. Adolescents (teenagers) drink too much soda. _____ T _____ F

3. What is the biggest health problem for children in the U.S.? Is it unhealthy diet or not enough exercise? Do you think the children's health will get better or worse in the future? Why?

 Surfing THE **INTERNET**

Go to the Internet. Enter the address for a search engine such as google.com, msn.com, or yahoo.com. Enter the search words **New York Marathon.** Find the names of people who won the New York City Marathon in the past. What countries are they from? What other information can you find? Tell your class.

Optional Activity: What kind of exercise is good for you? Look up exercises that will make you healthier and reduce stress. Find more information about jogging or running for your health. Print out the information and share it with your class.

UNIT

4

REMARKABLE RESEARCHERS

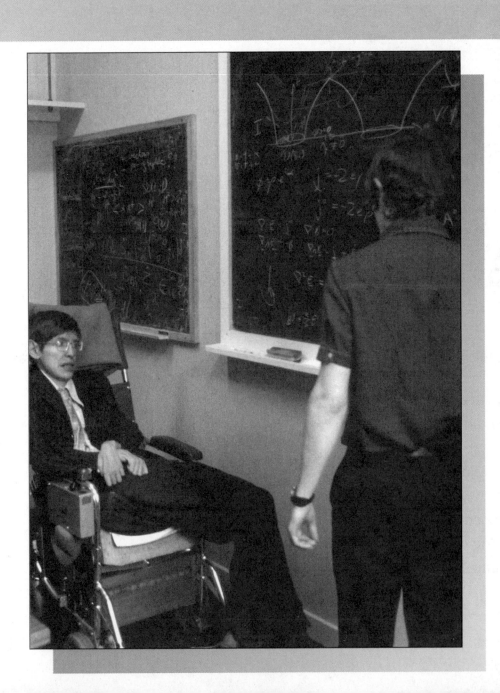

99

7

Margaret Mead: The World Was Her Home

Prereading Preparation

Work with a classmate to discuss these questions.

1. Look at the photograph above. The woman on the right was Margaret Mead. She was American.
   a. What was her occupation? What do you think?
      1. She was an artist.
      2. She was an anthropologist.
      3. She was a doctor.
   b. What kind of work did Margaret Mead do?
      1. She helped sick people.
      2. She painted pictures.
      3. She studied different cultures.

c. Where did Margaret Mead do most of her work?

    1. in her own country

    2. in a hospital

    3. in different countries

2. Describe the kind of work that you think Margaret Mead did. Write one or two sentences.

_____

_____

_____

3. Read the title of this chapter. Why do you think the whole world was Margaret Mead's home? How can the world be a person's home?

Directions: Read each paragraph carefully. Then answer the questions.

Margaret Mead: The World Was Her Home

Margaret Mead was a famous American anthropologist. She was born on December 16, 1901, in Philadelphia, Pennsylvania. She lived with her parents, her grandmother, and her brother and sisters. Her parents were both teachers, and her grandmother was a teacher, too. They believed that education was very important for children. They also believed that the world was important. Margaret learned many things from her parents and grandmother.

When she was a child, Margaret's family traveled often and lived in many different towns. Margaret was always interested in people and places, so she decided to study anthropology in college to learn about different cultures. At that time it was not very common for women to study in a university. It was even more unusual for women to study anthropology.

1. ____ True ____ False   Margaret Mead's parents were anthropologists.

2. What do these two paragraphs discuss?
    a. Margaret's education as a young child
    b. the importance of Margaret's family and childhood
    c. the importance of Margaret's occupation

3. Why did Margaret decide to study anthropology?

    _____

4. What do you think the next part of the passage will discuss?

    _____

Margaret graduated from college in 1923. She wanted to continue her education in anthropology, so she decided to go to American Samoa to study about young women there. Many people did not know about the culture of American Samoa. Margaret wanted to learn about Samoans so that the world could learn about them, too.

Margaret lived in Samoa for nine months and learned the language. She talked with the Samoan people, especially the teenage girls. She ate with them, danced with them, and learned many details about their peaceful culture.

5. _____ True _____ False   Margaret went to Samoa to continue her education in anthropology.

6. Why did Margaret want to learn about the Samoan culture?
    a. She wanted to go to college in Samoa.
    b. She wanted to teach the world about Samoa.
    c. She wanted to learn the Samoan language.

7. How long did Margaret live in Samoa? _____

8. _____ True _____ False   Margaret knew the Samoan language before she went to Samoa.

9. She talked with the Samoan people, **especially** the **teenage girls.**

   a. **Especially** means

      1. only
      2. most importantly
      3. except for

   b. **Teenage girls** are

      1. girls from 13 to 19 years old
      2. girls from 7 to 14 years old
      3. girls over 18 years old

10. _____ True _____ False   The Samoan culture was peaceful.

When Margaret returned to the United States, she wrote a book about the young Samoan women she studied. The book was called *Coming of Age in Samoa,* and it was very popular. As a result, Margaret Mead became very famous. Before Margaret wrote her book, not many people were interested in anthropology. Because of Margaret's book, anthropology became a popular subject.

Margaret Mead studied many different cultures in her life. She continued to work, travel, write, and teach until she died in 1978. She was a remarkable woman of the world.

11. ***Coming of Age in Samoa*** was

    a. a book
    b. a magazine
    c. a teenage girl

12. What was the subject of Margaret's book?

    _____

13. Why did Margaret Mead become famous?

    a. because she was an anthropologist
    b. because she studied many cultures
    c. because she wrote a popular book

14. Margaret Mead continued to work, travel, write, and teach **until** she died in 1978.

    a. **Until** means

        1. when something begins

        2. when something continues

        3. when something stops

    b. Complete the following sentence.
       Last night Elizabeth studied at the library until

        1. it opened

        2. it closed

        3. she woke up

15. Margaret Mead was a **remarkable** woman of the world. **Remarkable** means

    a. educated

    b. hard-working

    c. unusual

Directions: Read the complete passage. When you are finished, answer the questions that follow.

Margaret Mead: The World Was Her Home

1   Margaret Mead was a famous American anthropologist. She was born on
2 December 16, 1901, in Philadelphia, Pennsylvania. She lived with her parents, her
3 grandmother, and her brother and sisters. Her parents were both teachers, and
4 her grandmother was a teacher, too. They believed that education was very
5 important for children. They also believed that the world was important.
6 Margaret learned many things from her parents and grandmother.
7   When she was a child, Margaret's family traveled often and lived in many
8 different towns. Margaret was always interested in people and places, so she
9 decided to study anthropology in college to learn about different cultures. At
10 that time it was not very common for women to study in a university. It was even
11 more unusual for women to study anthropology.
12   Margaret graduated from college in 1923. She wanted to continue her educa-
13 tion in anthropology, so she decided to go to American Samoa to study about
14 young women there. Many people did not know about the culture of American
15 Samoa. Margaret wanted to learn about Samoans so that the world could learn
16 about them, too.

17   Margaret lived in Samoa for nine months and learned the language. She
18 talked with the Samoan people, especially the teenage girls. She ate with them,
19 danced with them, and learned many details about their peaceful culture.

20   When Margaret returned to the United States, she wrote a book about the
21 young Samoan women she studied. The book was called *Coming of Age in Samoa*,
22 and it was very popular. As a result, Margaret Mead became very famous. Before
23 Margaret wrote her book, not many people were interested in anthropology.
24 Because of Margaret's book, anthropology became a popular subject.

25   Margaret Mead studied many different cultures in her life. She continued to
26 work, travel, write, and teach until she died in 1978. She was a remarkable
27 woman of the world.

A.   Scanning for Information

Read the following questions. Then go back to the complete passage and scan quickly for the answers. Write them in the space under each question.

1. Margaret Mead decided to study anthropology in college to learn about different cultures.

   a. Why do you think she made this decision?

   _____

   _____

   b. Was this an unusual decision? Why or why not?

   _____

   _____

2. How did Margaret study the Samoan people?

   _____

   _____

3. What did Margaret Mead contribute to anthropology? In other words, why was Margaret Mead important to anthropology?

   _____

4. What is the main idea of this passage?

   _____

   _____

In English, some verbs (v.) become nouns (n.) by adding the suffix *-ence* or *-ance* to the verb. Read the following sentences. Decide if the correct word is a noun or a verb. Circle your answer.

1. Children <u>depend / dependence</u> on their parents for everything.
        (v.)   (n.)

2. This <u>depend / dependence</u> usually continues until they complete high
        (v.)   (n.)

   school.

3. Eric's <u>appears / appearance</u> changed in many ways as he became older.
        (v.)   (n.)

4. For example, he <u>appears / appearance</u> thinner, and his hair is turning gray.
        (v.)   (n.)

5. My sister and I <u>differ / difference</u> from each other in many ways.
        (v.)   (n.)

6. Because of our <u>differ / differences</u>, we are not very close.
        (v.)   (n.)

7. Sharks prefer warm water. They <u>avoid / avoidance</u> cold water.
        (v.)   (n.)

8. Their <u>avoid / avoidance</u> of cold water helps them to survive.
        (v.)   (n.)

Vocabulary in Context

Read the following sentences. Choose the correct answer for each sentence. Write your answer in the blank space. Use each word only once.

> especially (*adv.*)   remarkable (*adj.*)   believe (*v.*)

1. Helen enjoys all her classes, but she _____ likes her English class. That is her favorite subject.

2. My brother and I exercise every day. We _____ that exercise is important for good health.

3. Sharks are _____ animals. They hunt for food at night by feeling vibrations in the water.

> cultures (*n.*)   peaceful (*adj.*)   as a result

4. The Samoans are very _____ people. They rarely disagree or fight with each other.

5. Choi and Marina come from different _____, but they are very good friends.

6. Maria did not do her homework last night. _____, she was not prepared for class today.

> until (*prep.*)   interested (*adj.*)   details (*n.*)   popular (*adj.*)

7. That is a very _____ type of car. Many people buy it because it is inexpensive and reliable.

8. Cesar is _____ in medicine. He wants to become a doctor.

9. I studied last night _____ midnight. Then I went to sleep.

10. There was an earthquake in California this morning, but I don't know the _____. I want to listen to the radio to learn more about it.

1. Refer back to the Prereading section. Read your description of the work that you thought Margaret Mead did. How accurate was your description?

2. Work with two or three partners. Imagine that you are a team of anthropologists. You are going to a different country to study a different culture. You plan to interview the people there to learn about their culture. What special features of this culture do you want to learn most about? What questions can you ask to get this information? Together, make a list of questions for your interview. When you are finished, write your questions on the blackboard. Discuss all the groups' questions and, as a class, make up one questionnaire.

3. Use your questionnaire to interview someone from a culture that is different from your own. You may interview someone in your class, but a person outside your class would be better. Bring the answers back to class. Discuss what you learned from your interview about this person's culture.

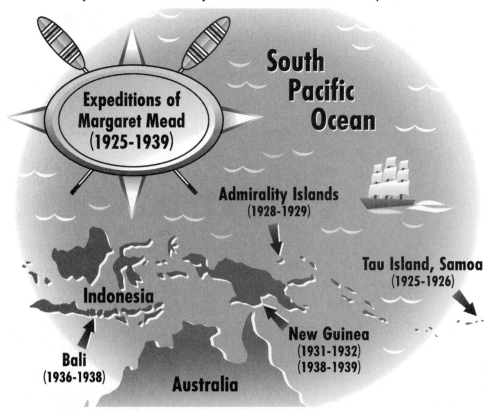

Topics FOR *Discussion* AND *Writing*

1. Describe one or two interesting things you have learned about American culture. Write a paragraph. How did you learn these things about American culture?

2. Describe someone important in your culture. This may be someone who is alive now or who lived in the past. Write a paragraph about this person. When you are finished, give your description to a classmate and read your classmate's description of an important person in his or her culture. Then discuss what you learned about your classmate's culture by reading about this person.

3. Do you think anthropology is important? Why or why not? Write a paragraph to explain your opinion. Give some examples.

4. Write in your journal. Imagine that you are a student of anthropology. Decide what culture you want to study. Discuss your reasons in a paragraph.

Crossword Puzzle

Read the clues on the next page. Write the answers in the correct spaces in the puzzle.

Crossword Puzzle Clues

Across

1. Margaret Mead went to _____ at a time when it was not common for women to go to a university.

4. Margaret Mead was a very _____ person. Many people knew her and read her books.

7. Margaret Mead was an _____.

12. Margaret Mead studied different people and their _____.

13. Because of Margaret Mead, many people became very _____ in learning about other cultures.

14. American _____ was the first country Margaret Mead went to and studied.

15. Margaret Mead studied many _____ about people's lives, such as what they ate.

16. Margaret Mead learned to _____ other languages.

Down

2. Margaret Mead was interested in other people, _____ young women and their lives.

3. Margaret Mead traveled all over the _____.

5. Margaret Mead wrote many _____ about the cultures she studied.

6. Margaret Mead's first book made her _____.

8. It is _____ for everyone to understand other people's cultures.

9. Today it is not _____ for women to go to a university to study anthropology.

10. Because of all she did in her life, Margaret Mead was a very _____ woman.

11. The first culture that Margaret Mead studied was very _____. These people were very gentle.

Read the passage below. Fill in each space with the correct word from the list. Use each word only once.

about	decided	graduated	study
culture	education	learn	

Margaret _____ from college in 1923. She wanted to con-
                    (1)
tinue her _____ in anthropology, so she _____ to
              (2)   (3)
go to American Samoa to _____ the young women there. Many
                            (4)
people did not know about the _____ of American Samoa.
                                  (5)
Margaret wanted to learn _____ Samoans so that the world
                            (6)
could _____ about them, too.
          (7)

because	interested	result	subject
book	popular	returned	wrote

When Margaret _____ to the United States from Samoa, she
                    (8)
_____ a book about the young Samoan women she studied.
      (9)
The _____ was called *Coming of Age in Samoa,* and it was very
        (10)
_____ . As a _____ , Margaret Mead became very
      (11)   (12)
famous. Before Margaret wrote her book, not many people were

_____ in anthropology. _____ of Margaret's book,
      (13)   (14)
anthropology became a popular _____ , and many people began
                                  (15)
to read about different cultures.

Louis Pasteur: A Modern-Day Scientist

Prereading Preparation

Work with a classmate to discuss these questions.

1. Look at the picture. This man was Louis Pasteur.

   a. What kind of scientific work did he do? What do you think?
      1. He was an inventor.
      2. He was a chemist.
      3. He was a medical doctor.
   b. Where did Louis Pasteur do his work?
      1. in a laboratory
      2. in a hospital
      3. in an office
2. Read the title of this chapter.
   a. How is modern scientific work different from scientific work that people did hundreds of years ago?
   b. Why do you think Louis Pasteur was a modern-day scientist?

Directions: Read each paragraph carefully. Then answer the questions.

Louis Pasteur: A Modern-Day Scientist

In the summer of 1885, 9-year-old Joseph Meister was a very ill little boy. He had been attacked by a sick dog that had rabies, a deadly disease. His doctor tried to help him, but there was no cure for rabies at that time. The doctor told Joseph's parents that perhaps there was one man who could save Joseph's life. His name was Louis Pasteur.

---

1. A **disease** is
   a. a summer activity
   b. an attack by an animal
   c. an illness; a sickness

2. What is rabies?

   _____

3. Did Joseph have rabies?
   a. Yes
   b. No

4. a. Was Joseph's doctor able to help him? _____
   b. Why or why not?

   _____

5. A **cure** for a disease is
   a. a medicine or treatment that makes an illness go away
   b. a careful description of that disease in a book
   c. a special doctor who knows about that disease

6. **His name was Louis Pasteur.** Who does this refer to?
   a. Joseph's parents
   b. Joseph's doctor
   c. the man who could save Joseph's life

7. What do you think the next paragraph will discuss?
   a. Joseph's life after he became well again
   b. the life of Joseph's doctor
   c. Louis Pasteur's life

When Pasteur was a young boy in France, he was very curious. Louis was especially interested in medicine, so he spent many hours every day with the chemist who lived in his small town. The chemist sold pills, cough syrups, and other types of medicine, just as modern pharmacists, or druggists, do today. At that time, the chemist had to make all the medicines himself. Young Louis enjoyed watching the chemist as he worked and listening to him assist the customers who came to him each day. Pasteur decided that one day he wanted to help people, too.

As a schoolboy, Pasteur worked slowly and carefully. At first, his teachers thought that young Louis might be a slow learner. Through elementary school, high school, and college, Pasteur worked the same thoughtful way. In fact, he was not a slow learner, but a very intelligent young man. He became a college professor and a scientist, and he continued to work very carefully.

8. Louis was **especially** interested in medicine, **so** he spent many hours every day with the chemist who lived in his small town.
   a. **Especially** means
      1. mostly
      2. probably
      3. originally
   b. **So** means
      1. because
      2. as a result
      3. all the time

9. Louis was a very **curious** person. He enjoyed watching the chemist as he worked and listening to the chemist **assist** his customers.

 a. **Curious** means
   1. very hard-working
   2. very careful
   3. very interested in learning

 b. **Assist** means
   1. help
   2. sell
   3. work

10. Why did Louis spend many hours with the chemist?

 a. Louis was interested in medicine.

 b. Louis wanted to become a chemist.

 c. The chemist needed Louis' help.

11. The chemist sold pills, cough syrups, and other types of medicine, **just as pharmacists,** or druggists, **do today.**

 a. **Just as** means
   1. only
   2. the same as
   3. whereas

 b. **Pharmacists** are _____ .

 c. What do pharmacists **do today?**

   _____

12. **As a schoolboy,** Pasteur worked slowly and carefully. **At first,** his teachers thought that young Louis might be a slow learner.

    a. **As a schoolboy** means

        1. Louis acted like a little boy

        2. when Louis was a boy in school

        3. boys in school always work slowly

    b. **At first** means

        1. in the beginning

        2. one time

        3. for one reason

    c. Why did his teacher think Louis might be a slow learner?

        _____

13. ____ True ____ False   Louis was a slow learner and not an intelligent man.

14. ____ True ____ False   Louis continued to work very carefully when he became a professor and a scientist.

15. What do you think the next part of the passage will discuss?

        _____

Because of Pasteur's patient methods, he was able to make many observations about germs. For example, germs cause meat and milk to spoil. They also cause many serious diseases. Pasteur was studying about the germs that cause rabies when Joseph Meister became ill. In fact, Pasteur believed he had a cure for rabies, but he had never given it to a person before. At first, Pasteur was afraid to treat Joseph, but his doctor said the child was dying. Pasteur gave Joseph an inoculation, or shot, every day for 10 days. Slowly, the child became better. Pasteur's vaccination cured him.

16. Why was Pasteur able to make many observations about germs?
    a. because he was very intelligent
    b. because he was patient
    c. because germs cause food to spoil

17. Germs cause meat and milk to **spoil.** Spoil means
    a. become warm
    b. become uneatable
    c. become cold

18. Why was Pasteur afraid to treat Joseph at first?
    a. He had never given the cure to a human before.
    b. He did not think he could cure rabies.
    c. His doctor said the child was dying.

19. a. What is an **inoculation?**
    _____

    b. **Every day for ten days** is
       1. ten shots every day
       2. one shot after ten days
       3. one shot each day for ten days

20. Why did the child become better?

    _____

    _____

During his lifetime, Pasteur studied germs and learned how they cause diseases in animals and people. He developed vaccinations that prevent many of these illnesses. He also devised the process of pasteurization, which stops foods such as milk from spoiling. Louis Pasteur died on September 28, 1895, at the age of 72. Modern medicine continues to benefit from the work of this great scientist.

21. **During his lifetime** means
    a. in the years that he lived
    b. after he became a college professor
    c. when Joseph Meister was ill

22. **Prevent** means
    a. describe something carefully
    b. help something happen
    c. stop something from happening

23. What can **vaccinations** do?
    a. help keep animals and people healthy
    b. cause illnesses
    c. stop food from spoiling

24. Pasteur **devised** the **process** of pasteurization.
    a. **Devised** means
       1. named
       2. invented
       3. liked
    b. A **process** is a
       1. medical treatment
       2. way to make money
       3. specific way of doing something
    c. **The process of pasteurization**
       1. prevents disease
       2. causes illnesses
       3. prevents milk from spoiling

25. **Modern medicine** continues to **benefit** from the work of this great scientist.

    a. **Modern medicine** means

        1. medicine in the past

        2. medicine today

        3. vaccinations

    b. When we **benefit** from something, we

        1. get an advantage

        2. get a disadvantage

Directions: Read the complete passage. When you are finished, you will answer the questions that follow.

Louis Pasteur: A Modern-Day Scientist

1   In the summer of 1885, nine-year-old Joseph Meister was a very ill little boy.
2   He had been attacked by a sick dog that had rabies, a deadly disease. His doctor
3   tried to help him, but there was no cure for rabies at that time. The doctor told
4   Joseph's parents that perhaps there was one man who could save Joseph's life.
5   His name was Louis Pasteur.

6   When Pasteur was a young boy in France, he was very curious. Louis was
7   especially interested in medicine, so he spent many hours every day with the
8   chemist who lived in his small town. The chemist sold pills, cough syrups, and
9   other types of medicine, just as modern pharmacists, or druggists, do today. At
10   that time, the chemist had to make all the medicines himself. Young Louis
11   enjoyed watching the chemist as he worked and listening to him assist the cus-
12   tomers who came to him each day. Pasteur decided that one day he wanted to
13   help people, too.

14   As a schoolboy, Pasteur worked slowly and carefully. At first, his teachers
15   thought that young Louis might be a slow learner. Through elementary school,
16   high school, and college, Pasteur worked the same thoughtful way. In fact, he
17   was not a slow learner, but a very intelligent young man. He became a college
18   professor and a scientist, and he continued to work very carefully.

19   Because of Pasteur's patient methods, he was able to make many observa-
20   tions about germs. For example, germs cause meat and milk to spoil. They also
21   cause many serious diseases. Pasteur was studying about the germs that cause
22   rabies when Joseph Meister became ill. In fact, Pasteur believed he had a cure for
23   rabies, but he had never given it to a person before. At first, Pasteur was afraid to
24   treat Joseph, but his doctor said the child was dying. Pasteur gave Joseph an
25   inoculation, or shot, every day for ten days. Slowly, the child became better.
26   Pasteur's vaccination cured him.

27   During his lifetime, Pasteur studied germs and learned how they cause dis-
28   eases in animals and people. He developed vaccinations that prevent many of
29   these illnesses. He also devised the process of pasteurization, which stops foods
30   such as milk from spoiling. Louis Pasteur died on September 28, 1895, at the age of
31   72. Modern medicine continues to benefit from the work of this great scientist.

Scanning for Information

Read the following questions. Then go back to the complete passage and scan quickly for the answers. Write them in the space under each question.

1. Why did Pasteur decide he wanted to help people?

    _____

    _____

2. Why did Pasteur agree to treat Joseph?

    _____

    _____

3. What were some of Pasteur's observations about germs?
    a. _____
    b. _____

4. What is the main idea of this passage?
    a. Louis Pasteur saved Joseph Meister's life by developing a cure for rabies.
    b. Louis Pasteur was a great scientist whose work continues to help science today.
    c. Louis Pasteur learned about germs and developed the process of pasteurization.

B.   Word Forms

In English, some verbs (v.) become nouns (n.) by dropping the final -e and adding the suffix -tion, for example, *graduate* (v.), *graduation* (n.). Read the following sentences. Decide if the word is a noun or a verb. Circle the correct answer.

1. Sociologists frequently <u>observe / observation</u> people in public places such
                     (v.)   (n.)
   as stores and parks.

2. Sociologists record their <u>observe / observations</u> in journals.
                 (v.)   (n.)

3. Claire's <u>educates / education</u> included music lessons.
        (v.)   (n.)

4. Claire's parents <u>educated / education</u> her to become a concert violinist.
           (v.)   (n.)

5. In the United States, children need to have certain <u>vaccinates / vaccinations</u>
                    (v.)   (n.)
   before they may begin school.

6. In the United States, doctors <u>vaccinate / vaccination</u> children for
           (v.)   (n.)
   several serious diseases.

7. Paige <u>continued / continuation</u> to study after she graduated from college.
       (v.)   (n.)

8. Paige believed that the <u>continued / continuation</u> of her education was
           (v.)   (n.)
   very important.

Vocabulary in Context

Read the following sentences. Choose the correct answer for each sentence. Write your answer in the blank space.

at first	because of	cure (*n.*)	decided (*v.*)

1. Don was very sick last year. _____ his long illness, he missed two months of school.

2. Maria didn't speak English when she came to the United States. _____ she didn't understand everyone, but gradually, she learned to communicate very well.

3. Last year, Monica _____ to change her job because she wasn't happy with her work.

4. Doctors do not have a _____ for the common cold, but they do for many serious diseases.

assisted (*v.*)	careful (*adj.*)	for example	process (*n.*)

5. Alexandra is always very _____ when she walks across the street. She looks in both directions for cars.

6. Making paper is a simple _____.

7. Three nurses _____ the doctor during the child's medical treatment.

8. Modern pharmacies sell many different products in addition to medicine. _____, they sell magazines, candy, toys, and cards.

caused (v.)	curious (adj.)	in fact

9. Our college basketball team is very good. _____, the team lost only one game last year.

10. Cats are very _____ animals. They are interested in looking at everything.

11. Last winter, the ice on the roads _____ many car accidents.

1. Louis Pasteur's discovery of a rabies vaccine saved many lives. What other discoveries help to save lives today? Work in small groups with your class-mates, and discuss your ideas. Then complete the chart below. When you are finished, compare your chart with your other classmates' charts. As a class, discuss these discoveries. Decide which discovery is the most impor-tant one.

Discoveries	Illnesses Cured
rabies vaccine	rabies

2. Pasteur developed the process of pasteurization 100 years ago to make milk safe to drink. Today we know many other ways to prevent food from spoiling. Work with one or two classmates. Talk about some of these ways. Make a list and compare it with your other classmates' lists. Discuss which way is the most important, and why.

Topics FOR *Discussion* AND *Writing*

1. Look at the follow-up activity on page 128. Which discovery do you think is the most important? Write a paragraph. Tell why this discovery is important. Describe how it has helped people.

2. Many medical discoveries will be made in the future. What do you think will be the most important cure? Why? Discuss your ideas with your classmates. Decide which cures are the most important. Give your reasons.

3. Write in your journal. Think of a time when you or someone you know was not well. Describe the situation. What treatment helped this person? How did it help?

F.   Crossword Puzzle

Read the clues on the next page. Write the answers in the correct spaces in the puzzle.

Crossword Puzzle Clues

Across

2. Pasteur worked slowly and carefully. He was a very _____ man.

3. Some illnesses kill people. These diseases are _____.

4. After class, the students _____ home.

5. Aspirin and cough syrup are types of _____.

9. At first, Pasteur did _____ want to inoculate Joseph Meister.

10. Germs cause milk to _____.

12. People who want to know all about many things are very _____.

16. Joseph Meister was dying, _____ Pasteur inoculated him, even though he was afraid.

17. Pasteur discovered the _____ for rabies. His vaccination saved many people from rabies.

18. Ill; not well

19. We all _____ from medical discoveries.

20. The past tense of **eat**

21. There is a _____ for many types of diseases.

23. Pasteur did not live in a big city. He lived in a small _____.

25. Pasteur died _____ 1895.

Down

1. Many people _____ alive today because of Pasteur's vaccine.

2. A _____, or druggist, prepares medicine.

3. Pasteur _____ his work slowly and carefully.

4. _____ can cause disease.

6. People who shop in stores are called _____.

7. Each; every

8. We protect ourselves against some diseases with an _____, or shot.

11. Pasteur was born _____ 1823.

12. We _____ buy medicine in a drugstore, or pharmacy.

13. _____ is a serious disease. We can get it from an animal bite.

14. Pasteur liked to _____, or help, the druggist.

15. Vaccinations help _____ many kinds of illnesses.

21. Vaccinations are _____ important for children.

22. Pasteur was a professor. He was a scientist, _____.

24. You and I

G.   Cloze Quiz

Read the following paragraphs. Fill in each space with the correct word from the list. Use each word only once.

became	carefully	school	thoughtful
but	learner	scientist	

As a schoolboy, Pasteur always worked slowly and _____(1). At first, his teachers thought that young Louis might be a slow _____(2). Through elementary school, high _____(3), and college, Pasteur worked the same _____(4) way. In fact, he was not a slow learner, _____(5) a very intelligent young man. He _____(6) a college professor and a _____(7), and he continued to work very carefully.

age	devised	illnesses	studied
benefit	during	prevent	such

_____(8) his lifetime, Pasteur _____(9) germs, and learned how they cause _____(10) in animals and people. He developed vaccinations that _____(11) many diseases. He also _____(12) the process of pasteurization, which stops foods _____(13) as milk from spoiling. Louis Pasteur died on September 28, 1895, at the _____(14) of 72. Modern medicine continues to _____(15) from the work of this great scientist.

1. Do you think doctors prefer to work in big cities or small towns? Why?

2. Read the questions. Then watch the video and answer them.

   1. How old is Dr. Clark?
   - a. 44
   - b. 65
   - c. 73

   2. On the average day, how many hours of sleep does he get?
   - a. one to two
   - b. three to four
   - c. seven to eight

   3. How many days a week does he work?
   - a. five
   - b. six
   - c. seven

   4. Does Dr. Clark always get paid for his work?   Yes ____ No ____

3. In your opinion, does Dr. Clark like his job? How do the people in his town feel about Dr. Clark? Why? What has he done for the people and the town?

Surfing THE INTERNET

Now you know the names of two important researchers: Mead and Pasteur. Choose one researcher and search for more information about his or her life. Take some notes and tell your partner or your class what you learned.

Optional Activity: Use the Internet to learn about a researcher, an explorer, or a scientist you are interested in. Look this person up on the Internet. What things did this person discover? Print out a picture of this person and tell your class about your research.

UNIT 5

SCIENCE AND HISTORY

The Origin of the Moon

Prereading Preparation

1. What do you know about the moon? Work with your teacher and your classmates. Try to answer the following questions.

Questions	Answers
How far is the Earth from the moon?	
How old is the moon?	
Does the moon have an atmosphere?	
Where did the moon come from?	
Is there life on the moon?	

Directions: Read each paragraph carefully. Then answer the questions.

The Origins of the Moon

For thousands of years, people have looked up at the night sky and looked at the moon. They wondered what the moon was made of. They wanted to know how big it was and how far away it was. One of the most interesting questions was "Where did the moon come from?" No one knew for sure. Scientists developed many different theories, or guesses, but they could not prove that their ideas were correct.

Then, between 1969 and 1972, the United States sent astronauts to the moon. They studied the moon and returned to Earth with rock samples. Scientists have studied these pieces of rock, the moon's movements, and information about the moon and the Earth. They can finally answer questions about the origin of the moon.

1. **People wondered what the moon was made of.** When people looked at the moon, they felt
   a. curious
   b. afraid
   c. cold

2. _____ True _____ False   Thousands of years ago, people knew how big the moon is.

3. _____ True _____ False   Thousands of years ago, people knew how far away the moon is from the Earth.

4. Scientists developed many different **theories,** or guesses, but they could not prove that their ideas were correct.
   a. A **theory** is
      1. a correct idea
      2. something you already proved
      3. a guess
   b. Scientists had
      1. an idea that they were sure about
      2. an idea that they were not sure about

5. **Astronauts** are people who

    a. study rocks

    b. travel in space

    c. live on the moon

6. ____ True   ____ False   Scientists think that they know the origin of the moon.

7. What do you think the next paragraph will discuss?

_____

Today most scientists believe that the moon formed from the Earth. They think that a large object hit the Earth early in its history. Perhaps the object was as big as Mars. When the object hit the Earth, huge pieces of the Earth broke off. These pieces went into orbit around the Earth. After a brief time, the pieces came together and formed the moon.

This "impact theory" explains many facts about the Earth and the moon. For example, the moon is very dry because the impact created so much heat that it dried up all the water. The Earth has iron in its center. However, the moon has very little iron in its center. This is because the moon formed from lighter materials that make up the outer part of the Earth. Finally, the Earth and the moon are almost the same age: the Earth is about 4.5 billion years old, and the moon is about 4.4 billion years old.

8. Scientists think that a large object hit the Earth **early in its history.** When the object hit the Earth,

    a. people saw it happen

    b. the Earth was new

    c. people wrote about it

9. An **orbit** is

    a. a path or route around something in space

    b. a large distance in space

    c. a large rock in space

10. An **impact** means
    a. an object moves past another object
    b. an object hits another object

11. Scientists believe that in the past,
    a. the moon was part of the Earth
    b. the moon was close to Mars
    c. the moon hit the Earth

12. Scientists believe that
    a. the moon was always in one piece
    b. the moon is made up of many big pieces

13. The astronauts brought back pieces of rock from the moon. It is probably true that
    a. the rock from the moon is just like rock on Earth
    b. the rock from the moon is different from rock on Earth

14. The "impact theory" describes
    a. scientists' belief about the size of the Earth and Mars
    b. scientists' belief about the origin of the moon

15. How many facts about the Earth and the moon are in this paragraph?
    a. two
    b. three
    c. four

16. Which statement is true?
    a. The Earth is 4.5 billion years old, and the moon is, too.
    b. The moon is 4.5 billion years old, but the Earth isn't.
    c. The Earth is 4.5 billion years old, but the moon isn't.

No one can prove that something really happened billions of years ago. In the future, new information will either support this theory or show that it is wrong. For now, scientists accept the impact theory because it explains what we know today about the Earth and the moon.

17. ＿＿＿ True ＿＿＿ False   Scientists are sure that their idea is correct.

18. **In the future, new information will either support this theory or show that it is wrong.** Information that supports the scientists' theory
   a. helps prove the theory is correct.
   b. helps prove the theory is wrong.

19. Scientists accept the impact theory because
   a. no one can prove that the impact theory isn't true.
   b. the information they have about the Earth and the moon supports the impact theory.

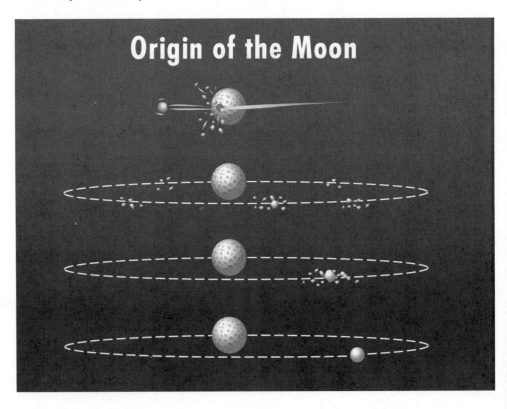

Origin of the Moon

The Origin of the Moon

1   For thousands of years, people have looked up at the night sky and looked
2 at the moon. They wondered what the moon was made of. They wanted to know
3 how big it was and how far away it was. One of the most interesting questions
4 was "Where did the moon come from?" No one knew for sure. Scientists devel-
5 oped many different theories, or guesses, but they could not prove that their
6 ideas were correct.

7   Then, between 1969 and 1972, the United States sent astronauts to the
8 moon. They studied the moon and returned to Earth with rock samples.
9 Scientists have studied these pieces of rock, the moon's movements, and informa-
10 tion about the moon and the Earth. They can finally answer questions about the
11 origin of the moon.

12   Today most scientists believe that the moon formed from the Earth. They
13 think that a large object hit the Earth early in its history. Perhaps the object was
14 as big as Mars. When the object hit the Earth, huge pieces of the Earth broke off.
15 These pieces went into orbit around the Earth. After a brief time, the pieces came
16 together and formed the moon.

17   This "impact theory" explains many facts about the Earth and the moon.
18 For example, the moon is very dry because the impact created so much heat that
19 it dried up all the water. The Earth has iron in its center. However, the moon has
20 very little iron in its center. This is because the moon formed from lighter mate-
21 rials that make up the outer part of the Earth. Finally, the Earth and the moon
22 are almost the same age: the Earth is about 4.5 billion years old, and the moon is
23 about 4.4 billion years old.

24   No one can prove that something really happened billions of years ago. In
25 the future, new information will either support this theory or show that it is
26 wrong. For now, scientists accept the impact theory because it explains what we
27 know today about the Earth and the moon.

Read the following questions. Then go back to the complete passage and scan quickly for the answers. Write them in the space under each question.

1. a. How many times did the United States send astronauts to the moon?

    1. one time
    2. three times
    3. We don't know.

    b. What did the astronauts bring back with them?

    _____

2. What kinds of information did scientists study in order to explain the origin of the moon?

    _____

    _____

    _____

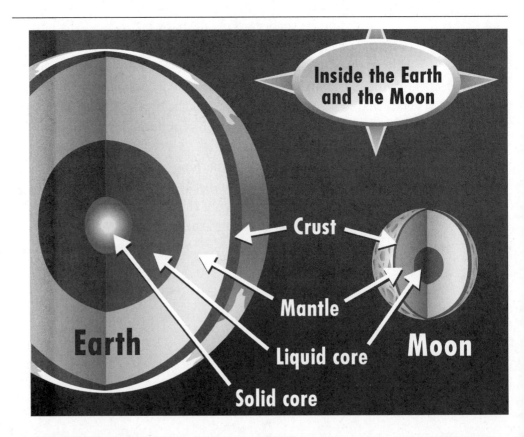

Inside the Earth and the Moon

Earth — Crust — Mantle — Liquid core — Solid core — Moon

3. a. Describe the **impact theory.**

   _____

   _____

   b. What are some facts about the Earth and the moon that this theory explains?

   _____

   _____

   c. How will future information affect this theory?

   _____

4. What is the main idea of this passage?
   a. The Earth and the moon are the same age.
   b. The impact theory is the best explanation of the moon's origin for several reasons.
   c. Scientists have developed different theories to explain the origin of the moon.

In English, some verbs (v.) become nouns (n.) by adding the suffix *-tion,* for example, *educate* (v.), *education* (n.). Sometimes there are spelling changes, too. Read the following sentences. Decide if each sentence needs a noun or a verb. Circle the correct answer.

1. The librarian <u>informed / information</u> me that the library is not open on
                (v.)   (n.)
   Sunday.

2. She gave me this <u>informed / information</u> over the telephone yesterday
                (v.)   (n.)
   morning.

3. Scientists believe that the <u>formed / formation</u> of the Earth and Mars
                     (v.)   (n.)
   happened at the same time.

4. The Earth and Mars <u>formed / formation</u> at the same time.
              (v.)   (n.)

5. Our teacher always <u>explains / explanations</u> the directions very clearly.
              (v.)   (n.)

6. We usually understand her <u>explains / explanations</u>.
                 (v.)   (n.)

7. Drug companies frequently <u>create / creation</u> new medicines.
               (v.)   (n.)

8. The <u>create / creation</u> of these new medicines takes a long time.
    (v.)   (n.)

C. Vocabulary in Context

Read the following sentences. Choose the correct answer for each sentence. Write your answer in the blank space.

| development (*n.*) | guess (*n.*) | support (*v.*) | wonder (*v.*) |

1. Henry told me his _____ about the origin of all the planets.

2. Many people _____ if there is life on other planets, such as Mars.

3. I know that the _____ of useful theories is very important.

4. Some scientific tests _____ Albert Einstein's theories about time.

| for now | in the future | then |

5. Travel to other planets is not possible right now, but _____ astronauts may travel to Mars or other planets.

6. Matt is only 14, so he has to ride his bicycle to school _____. However, when he becomes 17, he will be able to drive a car to school.

7. I plan to live in New York until I graduate from college. _____ I will move back to my country.

| but (*conj.*) | finally (*adv.*) | perhaps |

8. We wanted to go on vacation, but we didn't have enough money. We saved our money for two years, and we were _____ able to take a long vacation.

9. Max called Joyce on the telephone last night, _____ she wasn't home. He'll try to speak with her again today.

10. I don't know the directions to the bank. _____ my sister can give you that information. She knows the city very well.

1. Work with two or three people. Your group is going to send a spacecraft into space. Decide where it will go. Why do you want the spacecraft to go there? What do you want to find out about this place? Write your group's plan on the blackboard. Compare all the groups' plans. As a class, vote on which plan is best.

2. Some countries, such as the United States and Russia, are planning to build stations on the planet Mars. People will live and work there. Work with a group. Discuss the advantages and disadvantages of living on Mars. Make a list of both, and compare these with your other classmates. Decide if it is a good idea to send people to Mars to live and work.

Topics FOR Discussion AND Writing

1. Do you think it is important to study the moon and the planets? Why or why not? Write a paragraph describing your reasons.

2. Write in your journal. Some groups of people believe that there may be life on other planets. They are searching for signs of life. Do you agree that there may be life on other planets? Why or why not?

Crossword Puzzle

Read the clues on the next page. Write the answers in the correct spaces in the puzzle.

Crossword Puzzle Clues

Across

3. Scientists _____ the moon came from the Earth, but they do not have proof.

5. Scientists study the _____ of the moon around the Earth.

6. The sun is very _____, but the Earth is not.

7. The opposite of **no**

9. The moon is the brightest _____ in the night sky.

10. The opposite of **yes**

12. When we look _____ at the sky, we see the sun, the stars, the moon, and planets.

13. The distance _____ the Earth to the moon is about 250,000 miles.

15. New information may _____, or help prove, the scientists' belief.

18. The scientists may be _____, or incorrect.

19. Many scientists believe that the moon _____ from the Earth.

22. The past tense of **put**

23. People have several _____, or guesses, about the origin of the moon.

26. When a rock hits something hard, it can break into _____.

27. Astronomers are _____ who study the stars and planets.

29. The Earth and the moon are both about 4.5 _____ years old.

Down

1. The Earth has iron in its _____, or middle.

2. Scientists _____ a lot of information about the Earth and the moon.

3. Scientists believe that a large object hit the Earth and _____ into many pieces.

4. Scientists need more _____ about the Earth and the moon.

5. The Earth has one _____, but Mars has two.

6. Scientists believe that a large object _____ the Earth many millions of years ago.

8. We need a lot of information in order to _____ something that happened a long time ago.

11. The path, or route, that the moon takes around the Earth is called an _____ .

14. When one object hits another object, it _____ , or makes, heat.

15. **He, _____ , it**

16. Scientists cannot _____ their theory. They can only say that evidence supports it.

17. Maybe; possibly

20. When an object hits something, this is called an _____ .

21. People look up _____ the moon and think about it.

24. Scientists ask questions about the _____ of the moon. They also ask how the Earth was formed.

25. The present tense of **ate**

28. The _____ is the brightest object in the sky during the day.

30. The Earth _____ the only planet we know that has life.

G. Cloze Quiz

Read the following paragraphs. Fill in each space with the correct word from the list. Use each word only once.

around	dry	heat	moon	pieces
believe	facts	large	object	time

Today most scientists _____ that the moon formed from the
(1)
Earth. They think that a _____ object hit the Earth. Perhaps the
(2)
_____ was as big as Mars. When the object hit the Earth, huge
(3)
_____ of the Earth broke off. These pieces went into orbit
(4)
_____ the Earth. After a brief _____, the pieces
(5)   (6)
came together and formed the _____. This "impact theory"
(7)
explains many _____ about the Earth and the moon. For exam-
(8)
ple, the moon is very _____ because the impact created so
(9)
much _____ that it dried up all the water.
(10)

center	either	however	same	theory
Earth	future	prove	scientists	wrong

The Earth has iron in its center. _____, the moon has very lit-
(11)
tle iron in its _____. The moon formed from lighter materials
(12)
that make up the outer part of the _____. Finally, the Earth and
(13)
the moon are almost the _____ age: about 4.5 billions years old.
(14)
No one can _____ that something really happened billions
(15)
of years ago. In the _____, new information will
(16)
_____ support this theory or show that it is _____.
(17)   (18)
For now, _____ accept the impact _____ because it
(19)   (20)
explains what we know about the Earth and the moon.

Maps: The Keys to Our World

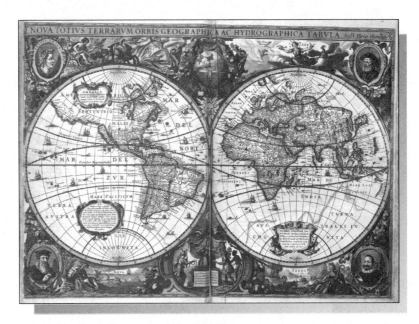

1636 Mercator World Map

Prereading Preparation

1. What is a map? Work in a small group. Write a definition of **map.** Write it in the box below. Then look up the word **map** in your dictionary. Write the dictionary definition in the box. Compare your definition with the dictionary's.

Your Definition of MAP	Dictionary Definition of MAP

2. Work in your group. Make a list of the different types of maps and their different uses.

Type of Map	Uses of this Type of Map
1. a street map	to help people find houses, stores, museums, or other buildings in a city
2.	
3.	
4.	
5.	

3. Read the title of this passage. How can maps be keys to our world? In other words, what do you think this passage will be about?

Directions: Read each paragraph carefully. Then answer the questions.

Maps: The Keys to Our World

We have street maps, bus maps, train maps, and road maps. We have maps of our countries, maps of the oceans, and maps of the world. We even have maps of other planets, such as Venus and Mars. These modern maps are very useful and important to us today, but maps are not a new invention. In fact, people have made and used maps for centuries.

1. People have made maps of everything: streets, countries, oceans, and planets. Why are maps so important to us? What do you think?

   _____

2. Modern maps are very useful and important to us today. **In fact,** people have made and used maps for centuries. What is the purpose of **in fact?**

   a. **In fact** introduces new information.

   b. **In fact** shows that the previous sentence is true.

   c. **In fact** shows that information is repeated.

3. What did maps look like hundreds of years ago? In other words, how were they different from maps we have today?

   _____

4. When do you think people began to make maps?

   _____ years ago

In Iraq, archaeologists discovered maps that are over 4,300 years old. These maps were made of clay. In China, archaeologists discovered silk maps that are 2,000 years old. However, historians believe that mapmaking in China is much older than 2,000 years. All these maps represented small areas, such as farm land and towns.

Archaeologists believe that the first map of the world may be a 2,600-year-old clay map from Babylonia (in modern Iraq). Ancient people did not know what the world really looked like, but they had many ideas about it. The Babylonian map shows the Earth as a flat circle. The circle contains a huge ocean with several islands in it. Other ancient maps showed the Earth on the back of a turtle, with four elephants holding the Earth up.

5. Archaeologists are people who
   a. have many ideas about what the world looks like
   b. study the life and culture of people who lived in the past
   c. make maps of the world from clay and silk

6. Historians believe that mapmaking in China is much older than 2,000 years. If this is true, why do you think historians didn't find older maps in China, but they did find older maps in Iraq?

   _____

7. Why did the oldest maps represent farms and towns? Why didn't the oldest maps represent the world? What do you think?

   _____

8. Read the ideas that ancient people had about the Earth. What did these people believe?
   a. They believed that the Earth was round.
   b. They believed that the Earth was flat.

9. What do you think the next paragraph will be about?

   _____

For centuries, people wondered how big the Earth was. Unfortunately, as long as they thought the Earth was flat, no one was able to figure out its size. Gradually, however, people began to realize that the Earth was really round.

Then, in the third century B.C. (2,300 years ago), a Greek man named Eratosthenes had an idea. Eratosthenes was sure that the Earth was a sphere. He used the sun and geometry to figure out the size of the Earth. He calculated that the circumference of the Earth was 28,600 miles (46,000 kilometers). The true size of the Earth is 25,000 miles (40,000 kilometers). Eratosthenes' measurement was wrong, but it was very close to the truth.

10. **As long as** people thought the Earth was flat, no one was able to **figure out** its size.
    a. **As long as** means
       1. very long
       2. the same size
       3. while
    b. **Figure out** means
       1. draw
       2. learn
       3. take out

11. **Gradually** means
    a. very slowly
    b. after 100 years
    c. scientifically

12. A **sphere** is a
    a. large shape
    b. planet
    c. ball

13. Eratosthenes used the sun and geometry to **figure out** the size of the Earth. He calculated that the circumference of the Earth was 46,000 kilometers.

a. What is a synonym for **figure out?**

    1. geometry

    2. kilometer

    3. calculate

b. Look at the three drawings below. Which one shows the circumference of the Earth?

    1.

    2.

    3.

14. A **measurement** is a

a. calculation

b. kilometer

c. true statement

For many centuries after Eratosthenes lived, people made maps of the Earth. However, they did not know very much about the world outside of Europe, Asia, and north Africa. Mapmakers could not draw accurate maps of the Earth until people began traveling around the world in the fifteenth century, mapping small areas each time. In the eighteenth and nineteenth centuries, people began making correct maps of countries, but the first accurate maps of the world were not made until the 1890s.

Maps today are reliable, inexpensive, and easy to understand. People depend on maps every day. What would our lives be like without them?

15. Why didn't people know much about the world for such a long time?

_____

16. **Accurate** means

a. big

b. small

c. correct

17. The **fifteenth century** is
    a. the time from 1401 to 1500
    b. the time from 1501 to 1600

18. How did people begin to learn about the world outside Europe, Asia, and north Africa?
    a. They took photographs of the other parts of the world.
    b. People lived in other parts of the world.
    c. People traveled and made maps of different areas.

Model of Babylonian Clay Tablet

Maps: The Keys to Our World

1.   We have street maps, bus maps, train maps, and road maps. We have maps
2. of our countries, maps of the oceans, and maps of the world. We even have maps
3. of other planets, such as Venus and Mars. These modern maps are very useful
4. and important to us today, but maps are not a new invention. In fact, people have
5. made and used maps for centuries.
6.   In Iraq, archaeologists discovered maps that are over 4,300 years old. These
7. maps were made of clay. In China, archaeologists discovered silk maps that are
8. 2,000 years old. However, historians believe that mapmaking in China is much
9. older than 2,000 years. All these maps represented small areas, such as farm land
10. and towns.
11.   Archaeologists believe that the first map of the world may be a 2,600-year-
12. old clay map from Babylonia (in modern Iraq). Ancient people did not know
13. what the world really looked like, but they had many ideas about it. The
14. Babylonian map shows the Earth as a flat circle. The circle contains a huge ocean
15. with several islands in it. Other ancient maps showed the Earth on the back of a
16. turtle, with four elephants holding the Earth up.
17.   For centuries, people wondered how big the Earth was. Unfortunately, as
18. long as they thought the Earth was flat, no one was able to figure out its size.
19. Gradually, however, people began to realize that the Earth was really round.
20.   Then, in the third century B.C. (2,300 years ago), a Greek man named
21. Eratosthenes had an idea. Eratosthenes was sure that the Earth was a sphere. He
22. used the sun and geometry to figure out the size of the Earth. He calculated that
23. the circumference of the Earth was 28,600 miles (46,000 kilometers). The true
24. size of the Earth is 25,000 miles (40,000 kilometers). Eratosthenes' measurement
25. was wrong, but it was very close to the truth.
26.   For many centuries after Eratosthenes lived, people made maps of the Earth.
27. However, they did not know very much about the world outside of Europe, Asia,
28. and north Africa. Mapmakers could not draw accurate maps of the Earth until
29. people began traveling around the world in the fifteenth century, mapping small
30. areas each time. In the eighteenth and nineteenth centuries, people began mak-
31. ing correct maps of countries, but the first accurate maps of the world were not
32. made until the 1890s.
33.   Maps today are reliable, inexpensive, and easy to understand. People
34. depend on maps every day. What would our lives be like without them?

Read the following questions. Then go back to the complete passage and scan quickly for the answers. Write them in the space under each question.

1. What are some map discoveries that archaeologists have made?

    a. _____

    b. _____

    c. _____

2. In the past, what shape did most people think the Earth had?

    _____

3. Describe the first map of the world.

    _____

4. a. Who calculated the circumference of the Earth?

        _____

    b. When?

        _____

    c. What did he think the circumference of the Earth was?

        _____

    d. Was his calculation correct?

        _____

5. When were the first reliable maps of the world made?

    _____

6. What is the main idea of this passage?

   a. The first maps were made thousands of years ago.

   b. Throughout time, maps have been important to people around the world.

   c. Maps are important to people today because they are very accurate.

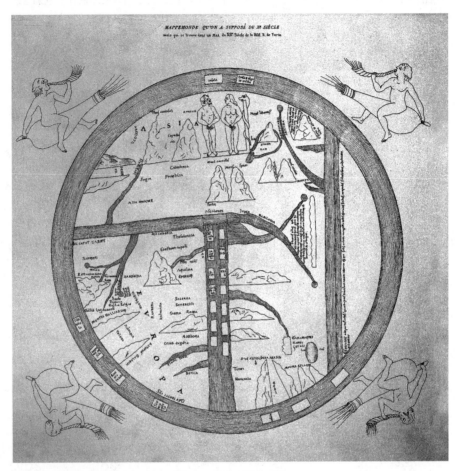

Tenth Century European Map of the World

In English, almost all adjectives become adverbs by adding the suffix *-ly,* for example, *correct* (adj.), *correctly* (adv.). Read the sentences. Decide if each sentence needs an adjective or an adverb. Circle the correct answer.

1. Years ago, cars were not <u>reliable / reliably</u>. They broke down often.
                                      (adj.)   (adv.)

2. However, cars perform very <u>reliable / reliably</u> today.
                                     (adj.)   (adv.)

3. You can eat <u>inexpensive / inexpensively</u> at the new Italian restaurant.
                          (adj.)   (adv.)

4. The restaurant offers very <u>inexpensive / inexpensively</u> lunches and
                                          (adj.)   (adv.)

   dinners on its menu.

5. Road maps are <u>easy / easily</u> to read.
                         (adj.) (adv.)

6. We can use road maps very <u>easy / easily</u>.
                                 (adj.) (adv.)

7. Suzanne did her math calculations <u>accurate / accurately</u>.
                                           (adj.)   (adv.)

8. She is always <u>accurate / accurately</u> with her figures.
                         (adj.)   (adv.)

C. Vocabulary in Context

Read the following sentences. Choose the correct answer for each sentence. Write your answer in the blank space.

gradually (*adv.*)   in fact   unfortunately (*adv.*)

1. Burt wants to go to the movies with us tonight. _____, he has to stay home and study for a math test.

2. I enjoy collecting old maps. _____, I have about 200 old maps in my collection.

3. Tina practiced the piano every day. _____, she became a very good pianist.

as long as   however   until

4. We want to write a composition. _____, we don't have any paper.

5. Harry never stops working _____ he finishes a job.

6. The children can play outside _____ it is daylight. They have to come inside in the evening.

calculated (*v.*)   realized (*v.*)   wondered (*v.*)

7. Ann left the party early. Bill _____ why she didn't stay later. He'll ask her tomorrow.

8. The computer _____ the answer more quickly than I did.

9. Ann _____ that the TV was broken when she tried to turn it on.

1. Refer to the list of maps and their uses that you made at the beginning of this chapter.

   a. What uses of maps did you write that are not mentioned in the first paragraph?

   b. What uses of maps are in the first paragraph but not on your list? Write these on your list.

2. The passage states that people began to realize that the Earth was really round. What do you think made people understand that the Earth was really round? Make a list of ideas or clues that you think helped people decide that the Earth was really round.

   a. _____

   b. _____

   c. _____

   d. _____

Topics FOR Discussion AND Writing

1. At the end of the reading, the author says that people depend on maps every day. Work with a partner. Make a list of the ways that people depend on maps. Compare your list with your classmates' lists. How many different ways do people depend on maps?

2. Write in your journal. At the end of the reading, the author asks what our lives would be like without maps. Describe an experience you had when you needed a map but didn't have one. Where were you? What happened? Write a paragraph about this event. When you are finished, work with one or two classmates. Read each other's stories. Decide whose experience was the most frightening, the funniest, or the most interesting. Then compare each group's favorite experience. As a class, decide on the most interesting experience.

Crossword Puzzle

Read the clues on the next page. Write the answers in the correct spaces in the puzzle.

Crossword Puzzle Clues

Across

1. Six hundred years ago, people thought that the Earth was _____, not round.

5. At first, people made maps of small _____ that they were famil- iar with.

7. Scientists _____ maps made of clay and silk.

8. We can buy maps of cities, countries, _____ the world.

10. Slowly, over time

12. Eratosthenes tried to _____ out the size of the Earth.

13. Each; every

16. Eratosthenes used geometry in order to _____ the size of the Earth.

17. The Earth is a _____, or ball.

20. **Me, her, _____, it, us, you, them**

21. Today, maps are very _____, or correct.

22. The past tense of **do**

24. We have _____ of the Earth, the moon, and some of the planets.

26. It is a _____ that the Earth is round.

27. Maps do not cost a lot of money. They are _____.

31. Babylonia is in the _____-day country of Iraq.

32. The past tense of **say**

Down

2. _____ are people who study past human life and culture.

3. The past tense of **have**

4. Maps _____ areas of the Earth such as cities.

6. To understand; to _____

9. Dependable

11. The opposite of **down**

12. The Earth is round. The Earth orbits the sun. These are _____ .

14. We have maps of other planets, such _____ Mars and Venus.

15. A circumference is a _____ of a round shape such as a ball.

18. Before photography, people used to _____ maps.

19. We _____ make very detailed maps today.

23. People rely on, or _____ on, maps every day.

24. **I, _____ ; she, her; he, him**

25. The Earth, Mars, and Venus are all _____ .

28. The past tense of **put**

29. The maps we have today are _____ detailed.

30. It is _____ true that the Earth sits on the back of a turtle.

Cloze Quiz

Read the following paragraphs. Fill in each space with the correct word from the list.
Use each word only once.

ancient	countries	first	invention	planets
centuries	even	ideas	maps	useful

   We have street maps, bus maps, train _____ (1), and road maps. We
have maps of our _____ (2), maps of the oceans, and maps of the world.
We _____ (3) have maps of other _____ (4), such as Venus and
Mars. These modern maps are very _____ (5) and important to us today,
but maps are not a new _____ (6). In fact, people have made and used
maps for _____ (7). Archaeologists believe that the _____ (8) map
of the world may be a 2,600-year-old clay map from Babylonia (in modern
Iraq). _____ (9) people did not know what the world really looked like,
but they had many _____ (10) about it.

accurate	began	draw	not	until
around	depend	inexpensive	time	without

   Mapmakers could not _____ (11) accurate maps of the Earth
_____ (12) people began traveling _____ (13) the world in the fifteenth century, mapping small areas each _____ (14). In the eighteenth
and nineteenth centuries, people _____ (15) making correct maps of
countries, but the first _____ (16) maps of the world were _____ (17)
made until the 1890s.

   Maps today are reliable, _____ (18), and easy to understand. People
_____ (19) on maps every day. What would our lives be like _____ (20)
them?

1. Check the words you know. Discuss the words you don't know.

    ____ moon   ____ space   ____ stars   ____ planet

    ____ sun   ____ astronaut ____ rocket   ____ comet

    ____ Earth   ____ telescope ____ satellite ____ meteor

2. Read the questions. Then watch the video and answer them.

    a. The Pictures of the Day website is compared to a place. What is the place?

        ____ space museum

        ____ art gallery

        ____ classroom

    b. "The _____ Factor" means that when the scientist sees the picture, he says "_____!" and knows right away he wants to use it on the computer.

        ____ Gee Whiz

        ____ Wow

        ____ Beauty

    c. Which of these pictures does the video show?

        ____ the Earth at night   ____ astronauts

        ____ the moon   ____ telescope

        ____ planets   ____ all of the above

3. The reporter says the Pictures of the Day are not just "eye candy." What does he mean? Why do you think people like to look at pictures of space?

surfing THE INTERNET

Learn more about space. Choose one of the words from Exercise 1 and type it into a search engine. Read about the object and tell your class what you learned about it.

Optional Activity: Search for *Astronomy Picture of the Day.* Click on **archive** to look at some of the pictures. Which ones do you like best? Print out your favorite picture and show it to your partner or your class. Use the picture to make a screen saver on your computer.

UNIT

FUTURE
TECHNOLOGY TODAY

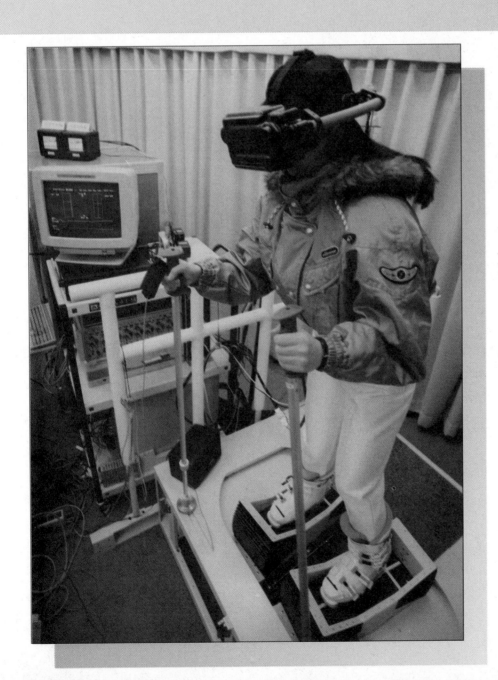

Saving Lives with Weather Forecasting

Prereading Preparation

1. What is weather forecasting? Who does it?

2. Look at the picture above. Work with a partner. What do you think happens to buildings when a tornado strikes? What are its effects? Describe them. Compare your description with your classmates' answers.

3. Read the title of this chapter. What do you think this passage will discuss?

Directions: Read each paragraph carefully. Then answer the questions.

Saving Lives with Weather Forecasting

On the night of April 25, 1994, a massive tornado struck the town of Lancaster, Texas. The tornado destroyed more than 175 homes. It also flattened the business district. Ordinarily, a tornado like the one that struck Lancaster kills dozens of people. Amazingly, only four people died.

1. **Massive** means
   a. destroy
   b. very big
   c. windy

2. _____ True   _____ False   The tornado destroyed the business district.

3. **Ordinarily** means
   a. usually
   b. really
   c. obviously

4. **Amazingly, only four people died.** This sentence means
   a. it is good that only four people died
   b. it is surprising that only four people died
   c. it is sad that four people died

Why did so few people die that night in Lancaster? Part of the reason is modern weather technology: **Next Generation Weather Radar,** or **Nexrad.** This sphere-shaped instrument identified the tornado a full 40 minutes before the tornado hit. As a result, weather forecasters were able to warn the people in the town. This advance warning helped many people to leave Lancaster before the tornado struck.

Nexrad is the first weather-service radar that can detect strong winds and rain, which are characteristic of severe thunderstorms and tornadoes. In the past, an obsolete radar system was used to predict such storms. Under this old system, warnings often depended on eyewitness reports. These reports gave people only about three minutes to prepare for the tornado.

5. What is **Nexrad**?

   _____

6. This advance warning helped many people to leave Lancaster before the tornado struck. **Advance warning** means
   a. to warn people before something happens
   b. to warn people after something happens

7. _____ True _____ False   Two characteristics of thunderstorms and tornadoes are wind and rain.

8. **Characteristic** means
   a. wind or rain
   b. reason or cause
   c. quality or trait

9. **Obsolete** means
   a. not useful
   b. very new
   c. very useful

Today, more than 100 Nexrad systems are in place in the United States. By the late 1990s, a total of 152 systems will be working throughout the country. In the past, many severe thunderstorms and tornadoes struck without warning. Weather forecasters could not predict all of them. In fact, they did not predict 33 percent of all thunderstorms and tornadoes. As a result of Nexrad, this percentage has decreased to 13 percent. When all the Nexrad systems are in place, this percentage will be even lower.

10. What years are **the late 1990s**?
    a. 1990–1993
    b. 1993–1996
    c. 1997–1999

11. How many Nexrad systems will be in place by the late 1990s?

    _____

12. As a result of Nexrad, this percentage has **decreased** to 13 percent. **Decrease** means
    a. become higher
    b. become lower
    c. stay the same

Tornadoes occur all over the world, but most often in the United States. One third of all U.S. tornadoes strike in Oklahoma, Texas, and Kansas. Alaska is the only state that has never had a tornado. A tornado may last from several seconds to several hours, and its winds may reach up to 300 miles per hour (500 kilometers per hour). Because tornadoes are so powerful and so destructive, it is important to be able to predict them accurately. Consequently, the Nexrad system will become an indispensable part of American weather forecasting.

13. ____ True ____ False   Tornadoes occur only in the United States.

14. ____ True ____ False   Tornadoes may last a short time or a long time.

15. Because tornadoes are so powerful and so destructive, it is important to be able to predict them accurately. **Accurately** means

    a. exactly

    b. carefully

    c. early

16. **Indispensable** means

    a. useful

    b. important

    c. necessary

17. **Consequently** means

    a. however

    b. as a result

    c. hopefully

Directions: Read the complete passage. When you are finished, you will answer the questions that follow.

Saving Lives with Weather Forecasting

1   On the night of April 25, 1994, a massive tornado struck the town of
2 Lancaster, Texas. The tornado destroyed more than 175 homes. It also flattened
3 the business district. Ordinarily, a tornado like the one that struck Lancaster
4 kills dozens of people. Amazingly, only four people died.

5   Why did so few people die that night in Lancaster? Part of the reason is
6 modern weather technology: Next Generation Weather Radar, or Nexrad. This
7 sphere-shaped instrument identified the tornado a full 40 minutes before the
8 tornado hit. As a result, weather forecasters were able to warn the people in the
9 town. This advance warning helped many people to leave Lancaster before the
10 tornado struck.

11   Nexrad is the first weather-service radar that can detect strong winds and
12 rain, which are characteristic of severe thunderstorms and tornadoes. In the past,
13 an obsolete radar system was used to predict such storms. Under this old system,
14 warnings often depended on eyewitness reports. These reports gave people only
15 about three minutes to prepare for the tornado.

16   Today, more than 100 Nexrad systems are in place in the United States. By
17 the late 1990s, a total of 152 systems will be working throughout the country. In
18 the past, many severe thunderstorms and tornadoes struck without warning.
19 Weather forecasters could not predict all of them. In fact, they did not predict 33
20 percent of all thunderstorms and tornadoes. As a result of Nexrad, this percent-
21 age has decreased to 13 percent. When all the Nexrad systems are in place, this
22 percentage will be even lower.

23   Tornadoes occur all over the world, but most often in the United States.
24 One third of all U.S. tornadoes strike in Oklahoma, Texas, and Kansas. Alaska is
25 the only state that has never had a tornado. A tornado may last from several
26 seconds to several hours, and its winds may reach up to 300 miles per hour
27 (500 kilometers per hour). Because tornadoes are so powerful and so destructive,
28 it is important to be able to predict them accurately. Consequently, the Nexrad
29 system will become an indispensable part of American weather forecasting.

Scanning for Information

Read the following questions. Then go back to the complete passage and scan quickly for the answers. Write them in the space under each question.

1. In lines 4 and 5, why was it amazing that only four people died?

   _____

   _____

2. How did Nexrad save lives?

   _____

   _____

3. Before Nexrad, how did many forecasters know that a tornado was coming?

   _____

   _____

4. Is it important to accurately predict tornadoes? Why or why not?

   _____

   _____

5. What is the main idea of this passage?
   a. Tornadoes occur all over the world, but most tornadoes strike the United States.
   b. There is a new weather system that can predict tornadoes and save lives.
   c. A massive tornado struck a town in Texas, but only four people died.

B. Word Forms

In English, some verbs (v.) become nouns (n.) by adding *-ence* or *-ance*. Read the sentences below. Decide if each sentence needs a verb or a noun. Circle the correct answer.

1. Carmen <u>avoided / avoidance</u> alcohol while she was pregnant.
      (v.)   (n.)

2. <u>Avoid / Avoidance</u> of alcohol is important for a healthy baby.
    (v.)   (n.)

3. Tornadoes are a rare <u>occur / occurrence</u> in New Jersey.
                    (v.)   (n.)

4. They rarely <u>occur / occurrence</u> in Hawaii, too.
              (v.)   (n.)

5. Joanne's <u>depends / dependence</u> on her car is a problem.
            (v.)   (n.)

6. Joanne even <u>depends / dependence</u> on her car to drive three blocks to
              (v.)   (n.)

   the store.

7. Some buildings <u>resist / resistance</u> high winds.
                (v.)   (n.)

8. This wind <u>resist / resistance</u> can save lives during a tornado.
            (v.)   (n.)

Read the following sentences. Choose the correct answer for each sentence. Write your answer in the blank space.

> indispensable (*adj.*)   obsolete (*adj.*)   severe (*adj.*)

1. Because most businesses use computers, typewriters have become
   _____.

2. Computers are _____ to most businesses. They could not operate without computers!

3. Danielle has a _____ cold. Her doctor told her to stay in bed for several days.

> accurately (*adv.*)   amazingly (*adv.*)   consequently (*adv.*)

4. Kristen did not study last night. _____, she was not prepared for the exam this morning.

5. My wristwatch keeps time _____. It is now exactly noon.

6. I saw a terrible car accident on the highway. _____, no one was hurt.

> decreases (*v.*)   destroyed (*v.*)   predicts (*v.*)   warned (*v.*)

7. As the temperature _____, the weather becomes colder.

8. The weather forecaster _____ a warm, sunny day for tomorrow. Let's all go to the beach!

9. Christina's mother _____ her not to play near the street.

10. During the thunderstorm, a huge tree fell and _____ my car.

Follow-up Activities

1. The following illustration shows how tornadoes are formed. Look at the four steps carefully. Then put the four descriptions in the correct order.

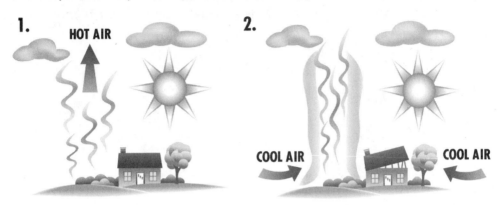

_____ Cooler air nearby rushes in to fill the space left by the rising hot air.

_____ As the Earth rotates, it causes the rotating motion in the air column. This process becomes stronger.

_____ The sun heats the ground. Columns of hot air rise where the ground is the hottest.

_____ This process speeds up and increases. It generates extremely high winds.

2. Tornadoes occur mostly in the United States. Work with a partner from your country. What kinds of severe weather (for example, hurricanes, typhoons, floods, blizzards) happen in your country? Make a list. Then write it on the blackboard. Join your country's list with other countries' lists. Make a chart of all the countries' severe weather.

3. It is important to be able to predict tornadoes in order to save lives. What other occurrences is it important to be able to predict? Work with two or three classmates. Make a list. Compare it with your other classmates' lists.

Topics FOR *Discussion* AND *Writing*

1. Nexrad is an important system because it can save lives. Think about another invention (for example, a smoke detector) that can save lives. Describe this invention. What does it do? Write a paragraph about it.

2. Many people listen to the weather forecast every day. Do you listen to it also? Why or why not? Do you think it is necessary every day? Write a paragraph about this.

3. Write in your journal. Did you ever experience severe weather (tornadoes, snowstorms, floods, etc.)? Write about this experience. If you did not experience bad weather yourself, write about what you read in a newspaper or heard about on television or radio.

Read the clues on the next page. Write the answers in the correct spaces in the puzzle.

Crossword Puzzle Clues

Across

1. Nexrad is a weather predicting _____ in the United States.

4. We _____ studying English.

6. We enjoy warm, sunny _____.

8. The past tense of **do**

11. The number of deaths from plane accidents has _____ recently. That's good news!

13. Modern technology is an _____ part of our lives. We cannot live and work without it.

16. Severe storms can be very _____. They flatten buildings and kill people.

18. Weather _____ are people who try to predict storms and other bad weather.

19. Every; each

21. The opposite of **no**

22. Many people try to _____ the future. They try to tell what will happen.

23. The present tense of **ate**

24. I am _____ that it will rain tomorrow. I am certain.

Down

1. New York is a _____ in the United States. California is a _____, too.

2. Nexrad is shaped like a _____. The Earth and the moon are this shape, too.

3. **I, _____; he, him; she, her; we, us**

5. Nexrad means "Next Generation Weather _____."

6. We heard a _____ on the radio that a severe thunderstorm is coming.

7. The past tense of **have**

9. _____, most people don't work on Saturday and Sunday in the United States.

10. John _____ speak two languages.

12. An airplane crashed in the mountains last night. _____, no one was killed.

14. We are coming to the _____ of this book. The next chapter is the last chapter.

15. Nexrad is very_____, or correct.

17. _____ are very powerful; they can destroy trees and buildings in a few minutes.

18. After a severe storm, some areas may be completely _____ because the buildings were destroyed.

20. Certain types of storms _____ only in particular parts of the world.

22. The past tense of **put**

Cloze Quiz

Read the following paragraphs. Fill in each space with the correct word from the list. Use each word only once.

characteristic	late	obsolete	predict	severe
eyewitness	lower	percentage	prepare	warning

Nexrad can detect strong winds and rain, which are _____ of severe
(1)
thunderstorms and tornadoes. In the past, an _____ radar system was used to
(2)
predict such storms. Under this old system, warnings often depended on
_____ reports. These reports gave people only about three minutes to
(3)
_____ for the tornado. Today, more than 100 Nexrad systems are in place in
(4)
the United States. By the _____ 1990s, a total of 152 systems will be working
(5)
throughout the country. In the past, many _____ thunderstorms and
(6)
tornadoes struck without _____. Weather forecasters could not
(7)
_____ all of them. In fact, they did not predict 33 percent of all thunderstorms
(8)
and tornadoes. As a result of Nexrad, this _____ has decreased to 13 percent.
(9)
When all the Nexrad systems are in place, this percentage will be even _____.
(10)

accurately	destructive	indispensable	only	tornado
all	hour	occur	several	weather

Tornadoes _____ all over the world, but most often in the United States.
(11)
One third of _____ U.S. tornadoes strike in Oklahoma, Texas, and Kansas.
(12)
Alaska is the _____ state that has never had a _____. A tornado
(13)   (14)
may last from several seconds to _____ hours, and its winds may reach up to
(15)
300 miles per _____ (500 kilometers per hour). Because tornadoes are so
(16)
powerful and so _____, it is important to be able to predict them
(17)
_____. Consequently, the Nexrad system will become an _____
(18)   (19)
part of American _____ forecasting.
(20)

12

Clues and Criminal Investigation

Prereading Preparation

1. What kinds of evidence can prove that a person committed a crime? Work with a partner. Look at the list of clues below and decide what type of crime these clues might help solve. Some clues may help solve more than one kind of crime. When you are finished, compare your work with your other classmates' work. Did you make the same decisions?

Clues		
blood	dirt	hair
bullets	fingerprints	pieces of glass
clothing fibers	footprints	a ransom note

2. Think of a crime that you heard about or read about. Describe it to your partner. What clues did the police use to help them solve this crime?

3. Read the title of this passage. What do you think the reading will be about?

Directions: Read each paragraph carefully. Then answer the questions.

Clues and Criminal Investigation

If you wanted to solve a crime such as a robbery or a murder, how would you start? What types of evidence would you look for? Crime experts all have a basic principle, or belief: a criminal always brings something to the scene of a crime and always leaves something there. As a result, crime experts always begin their criminal investigation with a careful examination of the place where the crime occurred.

1. A **crime expert** is
   a. a professional at committing crimes
   b. a professional at solving crimes

2. A **principle** is
   a. an idea that you have
   b. evidence that you have
   c. a belief that you have

3. What do crime experts think?
   a. They think that criminals are usually not very careful.
   b. They think that they can solve every crime that occurs.
   c. They think that they will always find clues at the scene of a crime.

4. What do you think the next paragraph will discuss?

   _____

When criminal investigators arrive at the scene of a crime, they look for evidence, or clues, from the criminal. This evidence includes footprints, fingerprints, lip prints on glasses, hair, blood, clothing fibers, and bullet shells, for example. These are all clues that the criminal may have left behind. Some clues are taken to laboratories and analyzed. For instance, fingerprints are "lifted" from a glass, a door, or a table. They are examined and compared by computer with the millions of fingerprints on file with the police, the Federal Bureau of Investigation (FBI), and other agencies.

5. The **scene of a crime** is
   a. a part of a movie
   b. the place where the crime occurred
   c. a description of the crime

6. a. **Evidence** means
   1. clues
   2. criminals
   3. beliefs

   b. Some examples of clues are

   _____

7. Fingerprints are "lifted" from a glass, a door, or a table. Then experts analyze them in a laboratory. In the first sentence, **lifted** means
   a. found
   b. taken
   c. examined

8. What will the next part of this reading discuss?

   _____

In the case of murder, experts examine blood and compare it to the blood of the victim. If the blood isn't the victim's, then it might be the murderer's. Furthermore, experts can analyze the DNA from a person's cells, such as skin cells. Like fingerprints, each person's DNA is unique, which means that everyone's DNA is different. These clues help to identify the criminal.

In some cases, a criminal uses a gun when committing a crime. Every gun leaves distinctive marks on a bullet when the gun is fired. The police may find a bullet at the scene or recover a bullet from a victim's body. Experts can examine the markings on the bullet and prove that it was fired from a specific gun. This clue is strong evidence that the owner of the gun may be guilty. Consequently, the police will suspect that this person committed the crime.

9. A **victim** is
   a. the person who committed the crime
   b. the person the crime is committed against

10. **Furthermore** means
    a. in addition
    b. farther away
    c. however

11. Like fingerprints, each person's DNA is **unique,** which means that everyone's DNA is different.
    a. **Unique** means
       1. from a person's body
       2. original; individual
       3. a special clue
    b. Which one of the following sentences is true?
       1. Each person's DNA and fingerprints are different from every other person's.
       2. Each person's DNA is different from every other person's, but their fingerprints are not.
       3. Each person's fingerprints are different from every other person's, but their DNA is not.

12. a. **Distinctive** means
    1. particular
    2. clear
    3. metal
   b. The markings on bullets fired from two different guns
    1. can sometimes be the same
    2. can never be the same

13. A gun's **owner** is
   a. the person who used the gun
   b. the person that the gun belongs to
   c. the person who found the gun

14. a. The police **suspect** that a person has committed a crime. This sentence means that
    1. the police are sure that a specific person has committed a crime
    2. the police believe that a specific person has committed a crime
   b. **Suspect** means
    1. think that something is true
    2. know that something is true

15. **Consequently** means
   a. in addition
   b. however
   c. as a result

Clues from the scene of a crime help the police identify a suspect. If other evidence supports these clues, then the police can charge the suspect with the crime. It is important to remember, however, that in the United States, a person is innocent until proven guilty in a court of law.

16. The police charge a person with a crime when
    a. they find a gun that belongs to that person
    b. they have blood and bullets from the scene of the crime
    c. they have evidence to show that the person may have committed the crime

17. a. The words **innocent** and **guilty**
    1. have the opposite meanings
    2. have the same meaning
    b. An **innocent** person
    1. committed a crime
    2. did not commit a crime
    c. A **guilty** person
    1. committed a crime
    2. did not commit a crime

Clues and Criminal Investigation

1　　　If you wanted to solve a crime such as a robbery or a murder, how would
2　you start? What types of evidence would you look for? Crime experts all have a
3　basic principle, or belief: a criminal always brings something to the scene of a
4　crime and always leaves something there. As a result, crime experts always begin
5　their criminal investigation with a careful examination of the place where the
6　crime occurred.

7　　　When criminal investigators arrive at the scene of a crime, they look for evi-
8　dence, or clues, from the criminal. This evidence includes footprints, finger-
9　prints, lip prints on glasses, hair, blood, clothing fibers, and bullet shells, for
10　example. These are all clues that the criminal may have left behind. Some clues
11　are taken to laboratories and analyzed. For instance, fingerprints are "lifted"
12　from a glass, a door, or a table. They are examined and compared by computer
13　with the millions of fingerprints on file with the police, the Federal Bureau of
14　Investigation (FBI), and other agencies.

15　　　In the case of murder, experts examine blood and compare it to the blood of
16　the victim. If the blood isn't the victim's, then it might be the murderer's.
17　Furthermore, experts can analyze the DNA from a person's cells, such as skin
18　cells. Like fingerprints, each person's DNA is unique, which means that every-
19　one's DNA is different. These clues help to identify the criminal.

20　　　In some cases, a criminal uses a gun when committing a crime. Every gun
21　leaves distinctive marks on a bullet when the gun is fired. The police may find a
22　bullet at the scene or recover a bullet from a victim's body. Experts can examine
23　the markings on the bullet and prove that it was fired from a specific gun. This
24　clue is strong evidence that the owner of the gun may be guilty. Consequently,
25　the police will suspect that this person committed the crime.

26　　　Clues from the scene of a crime help the police identify a suspect. If other
27　evidence supports these clues, then the police can charge the suspect with the
28　crime. It is important to remember, however, that in the United States, a person
29　is innocent until proven guilty in a court of law.

Scanning for Information

Read the following questions. Then go back to the complete passage and scan quickly for the answers. Write them in the space under each question.

1. What do all crime experts believe?

    _____

2. Why are fingerprints from the scene of a crime compared with the fingerprints on file with the police, the FBI, and other agencies?

    _____

3. If the blood found at the scene of a murder isn't the victim's blood, why might it be the murderer's blood?

    _____

4. Why are blood, skin, and fingerprints so important to crime experts?

    _____

5. What is the main idea of this passage?
    a. Criminals often leave many clues at the scene of a crime.
    b. Fingerprints and bullets are important evidence of crimes.
    c. Crime experts analyze a variety of clues to identify criminals.

B.   **Word Forms**

In English, some nouns (n.) become adjectives (adj.) by adding -*ful*. Read the sentences below. Decide if each sentence needs a noun (n.) or an adjective (adj.). Circle the correct answer.

1. Criminal investigators are very <u>skill / skillful</u>.
                                     (n.)   (adj.)

2. Their <u>skill / skillful</u> is very important in helping them solve crimes.
          (n.)   (adj.)

3. Gilda is unusually <u>success / successful</u> in her career.
                        (n.)   (adj.)

4. She achieved <u>success / successful</u> in only a few years.
                  (n.)   (adj.)

5. Roseanne gave her elderly mother a lot of <u>help / helpful</u> when she was sick.
                                               (n.)   (adj.)

6. Because Roseanne was so <u>help / helpful</u> to her mother, she felt better
                            (n.)   (adj.)

    quickly.

7. Jerry is always very <u>care / careful</u> when he paints his house.
                          (n.)   (adj.)

8. He takes a lot of <u>care / careful</u> not to spill paint on the carpets.
                       (n.)   (adj.)

Vocabulary in Context

Read the following sentences. Choose the correct answer for each sentence. Write your answer in the blank space.

| evidence (*n.*) | expert (*n.*) | principle (*n.*) | suspect (*n.*) |

1. Emily is the most likely _____ in the murder of her husband. The police think she may have killed him.

2. Sam is a police _____ on guns and rifles. He knows more about these weapons than anyone else in the police department.

3. A strong _____ in American law is that a person is considered innocent until proven guilty.

4. The police suspect that Jean committed the store robbery, but they don't have any _____ against her, so they have to let her go.

| consequently (*adv.*) | furthermore (*adv.*) | if (*conj.*) |

5. I would go on vacation _____ I had enough money, but I don't. Perhaps I'll take a vacation next year.

6. An eyewitness saw John steal a car. The police found the stolen car in John's garage. _____, the police arrested John and charged him with the crime.

7. I'm sure that Nelson didn't shoot Tom. Nelson and Tom are very good friends. Someone else's fingerprints were on the gun. _____, Nelson was out of town on business when Tom was shot.

investigated (v.)	occurred (v.)	suspected (v.)

8. When the FBI _____ the bank robbery, they found out that the robbers had left the country.

9. Ten murders _____ in Johnston City last year.

10. Everyone _____ that Fran had a lot of money, but no one was able to prove it.

1. Work with two or three partners. Imagine that you are a group of crime experts. The police have asked you to investigate the following crimes. What clues will you look for at the scene of each crime? What additional evidence will you try to get in order to identify a suspect for each of these crimes?

Type of Crime	Clues at the Scene of the Crime	Additional Evidence
a murder		
a kidnapping		
a house break-in		
a jewelry store robbery		

2. Work with one or two partners. Make up a crime and devise some evidence to leave "at the scene of the crime." Then have your classmates investigate your crime and try to solve it. When you have all finished, discuss your evidence. Which group had the best clues?

Topics FOR *Discussion* AND *Writing*

1. Work with two or three partners. Find a description of a crime in a book, magazine, or newspaper. Read the description of the crime, the clues, and the suspect. Decide if there is enough evidence to show this person is guilty in a court of law. Write a paragraph describing your decision. Then read another group's crime description and let them read your group's. After you have made a decision, meet with the other group. Read each other's paragraphs. Does your group agree or disagree with the other group's decisions about the two crimes? Discuss your decisions.

2. Write in your journal. Think about a crime you read about. Describe the crime. What happened? When and where did this crime take place? How did the police investigate it? What clues did they find? How did they solve the crime? Share your story with a classmate. Which crime was more difficult to solve? Why?

Crossword Puzzle

Read the clues on the next page. Write the answers in the correct spaces in the puzzle.

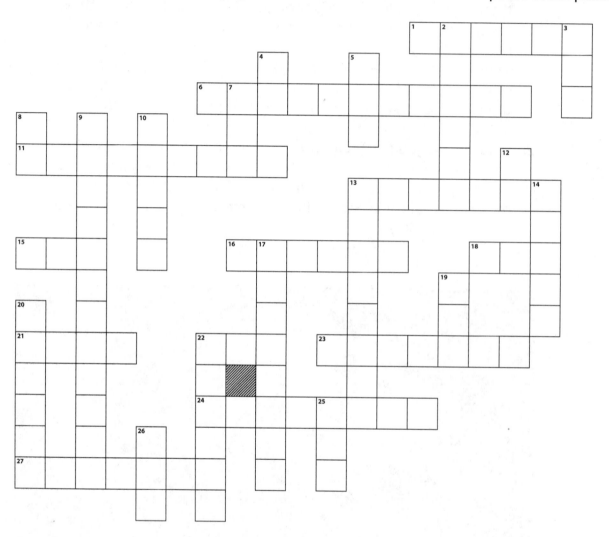

Crossword Puzzle Clues

Across

1. A gun leaves particular markings on a _____ .

6. My dog has _____ markings. He has a black leg, a black ear, and a black spot on his head.

11. I have a very simple _____ , or belief: I try my best with every-thing I do.

13. The police may ask many different _____ for help to solve a crime: chemists, dentists, etc.

15. We _____ doing a crossword puzzle.

16. John was the _____ of a robbery yesterday. Someone robbed him on the street.

18. Each; every

21. Uncommon; unusual

22. The past tense of **get**

23. Experts can _____ blood, hair, clothing, and other clues to a crime.

24. Mary did not steal John's wallet. She is _____ of that crime.

27. The police have a _____ in yesterday's bank robbery. They think they know who did it.

Down

2. Everyone's fingerprints are _____ . No two people have the same fingerprints.

3. Maria is studying English, and we are, _____ .

4. Robert is _____ tall as Gary. They are the same height.

5. Each person's _____ is unique, just like his or her fingerprints.

7. Sick; not well

8. The opposite of **down**

9. The lines on a person's fingers are _____ .

10. Crimes _____ , or take place, every day.

12. Our class ends _____ 10 o'clock.

13. The police don't have any _____, or clues, in this case yet.

14. Many specialists help the police _____ crimes.

17. The police look for clues, for _____, blood, hair, bullets, fingerprints.

19. The present tense of **said**

20. Murder, robbery, kidnapping, and car theft are all types of _____.

22. Tom was found _____ of stealing cars. The evidence against him was very strong.

25. We _____ do crossword puzzles.

26. The past tense of **let**

Cloze Quiz

Read the following paragraphs. Fill in each space with the correct word from the list. Use each word only once.

belief	case	evidence	leaves	result
careful	crime	furthermore	occurred	start

If you wanted to solve a _____(1)_____ such as a robbery or a murder, how would

you _____(2)_____? What types of _____(3)_____ would you look for? Crime

experts all have a basic principle, or _____(4)_____: a criminal always brings something

to the scene of a crime and always _____(5)_____ something there. As a

_____(6)_____, crime experts always begin their criminal investigation with a

_____(7)_____ examination of the place where the crime _____(8)_____. In the

_____(9)_____ of murder, experts examine blood and compare it to the blood of the

victim. _____(10)_____, experts can analyze the DNA from a person's cells, such as skin cells.

bullet	consequently	guilty	scene	suspect
clues	experts	gun	specific	uses

In some cases, a criminal _____(11)_____ a gun when committing a crime. Every

gun leaves distinctive marks on a bullet when the _____(12)_____ is fired. The police

may find a bullet at the _____(13)_____, or recover a bullet from a victim's body.

_____(14)_____ can examine the markings on the _____(15)_____ and prove that it

was fired from a _____(16)_____ gun. This clue is strong evidence that the owner of the

gun may be guilty. _____(17)_____, the police will _____(18)_____ that this person

committed the crime. All these clues may help police identify a suspect. If other evidence

supports these _____(19)_____, then the police can charge the suspect with the crime.

It is important to remember, however, that in the United States, a person is innocent until

proven _____(20)_____ in a court of law.

1. Tornadoes and hurricanes are hard to predict. Where do hurricanes occur?

2. Read the questions. Then watch the video and answer them.

   a. Forecasters give large storms and hurricanes names of people like Andrew or Emily. Which hurricanes does the video describe?

   ____ Opal ____ Brett ____ Camille ____ All of these

   b. Can forecasters predict when and where hurricanes will occur?

   ____ Yes ____ No ____ Not exactly

   c. Can forecasters stop hurricanes?

   ____ Yes ____ No ____ Sometimes

   d. How many people in hurricane areas have a hurricane plan?

   ____ 25% ____ 50% ____ 75%

3. What can people do to prepare for hurricanes? What things should they buy, for example? What other plans should they make?

Surfing THE INTERNET

Weather Forecasts

Enter the search words *weather* and the name of your city and state or country on the Internet. Check for today's weather forecast and temperature. Report the weather information to your partner or class. Are your forecasts the same or different?

Optional Activity: Go to the NOAA (National Oceanographic and Atmospheric Administration) website www.NOAA.gov. Read about some of the things NOAA does. Click on *Severe Weather Awareness* or *Cool NOAA Sites.* Print out an interesting picture from the *NOAA Photo Library* to show your classmates. Report what you learn to your partner or class.

INDEX OF KEY WORDS AND PHRASES

pasteurization 123
patient 38, 123
peaceful 106
perform 20
perhaps 38, 123, 141
pharmacists 123
physical education 73
pieces 141
pills 123
planets 159
popular 54, 87, 106
positive 38
powerful 177
predict 177
prefer 54
prevent 123
principle 195
process 121
prove 141, 195

Q
quiet 20

R
rabies 123
race 87
radar 177
raw 54
recently 87
record 38
recover 195
reliable 159
religious 54
remarkable 106
roller hockey 73
running 73., 87

S
sacred 54
Samoa 105, 106
Samoan 105, 106
sausages 55
scene 195
serious 123
septuplets 5
several 38, 159, 177
severe 177
shot 123
sick 123
silk 159
slowly 55, 87, 123
sociologists 54
solve 195
specific 195
sphere 159, 177
spoil 123
sports 73
step 38
strange 55
subject 106
support 141
suspect 195
systems 177

T
taste 54
tastes 55
team 73
technology 177
teenage 106
termites 55
theory 141
therefore 73

thoughtful 123
throw away 19
thunderstorms 177
together 19
too 19, 87, 105
tornado 177
treat 123
types 123, 195

U
unclean 54
unfortunately 159
unhealthy 73
unimportant 87
unique 195
until 104, 159, 195
unusual 5, 55, 87, 105
useful 159

V
vaccination 123
Venus 159
victim 195
video games 19

W
warn 177
warning 177
whole 87
wondered 141, 159

SKILLS INDEX